W9-CBU-226

ISSUES THAT CONCERN YOU

Activism

Jill Hamilton, *Book Editor*

GREENHAVEN PRESS
A part of Gale, Cengage Learning

GALE
CENGAGE Learning™

Detroit • New York • San Francisco • New Haven, Conn • Waterville, Maine • London

Christine Nasso, *Publisher*
Elizabeth Des Chenes, *Managing Editor*

© 2010 Greenhaven Press, a part of Gale, Cengage Learning

Gale and Greenhaven Press are registered trademarks used herein under license.

For more information, contact:
Greenhaven Press
27500 Drake Rd.
Farmington Hills, MI 48331-3535
Or you can visit our Internet site at gale.cengage.com

For product information and technology assistance, contact us at

Gale Customer Support, 1-800-877-4253
For permission to use material from this text or product, submit all requests online at
www.cengage.com/permissions

Further permissions questions can be e-mailed to permissionrequest@cengage.com

Articles in Greenhaven Press anthologies are often edited for length to meet page require-ments. In addition, original titles of these works are changed to clearly present the main thesis and to explicitly indicate the author's opinion. Every effort is made to ensure that Greenhaven Press accurately reflects the original intent of the authors. Every effort has been made to trace the owners of copyrighted material.

Cover image: Yellowdog Productions/Lifesize/Getty Images

LIBRARY OF CONGRESS CATALOGING-IN-PUBLICATION DATA

Activism / Jill Hamilton, book editor.
    p. cm. -- (Issues that concern you)
  Includes bibliographical references and index.
  ISBN 978-0-7377-4493-4 (hbk.)
  1. Youth--Political activity--Juvenile literature. 2. Social action--Juvenile literature.
I. Hamilton, Jill.
  HQ799.2.P6A29 2009
  323.3'52--dc22

                                          2009019031

Printed in the United States of America
1 2 3 4 5 6 7 13 12 11 10 09

CONTENTS

INTRODUCTION

Teens who are too young to drive or vote are still old enough to make a difference in the world. Young activists have played a big role in helping to improve the world. They have aided people in need, changed child labor laws, and even helped shape foreign policy.

An early example of a successful youth-led action in America's history is the newsboys strike of 1899. At the time cities were filled with young newsboys who sold papers on the street. The newsboys were poor, wore ragged clothing, and were often homeless. They worked long, hard hours trying to sell all of their papers, since the newspaper companies refused to buy back unsold papers. If the boys did not sell their papers, they might end up breaking even, or even losing money after a full day's work. When distribution costs rose, thousands of newsboys in New York, led by a boy called Kid Blink, went on strike against two prominent newspaper owners, William Randolph Hearst and Joseph Pulitzer. The strike lasted two weeks and ended with a victory for the strikers—the newspapers agreed to buy back the unsold papers.

The important lesson of this story is not that the boys got a few cents more a day, but that activism is a hugely powerful tool for social change. Think of the players in the story. At this time, there were few more powerful men in the country than Hearst and Pulitzer. Both were rich, well-known men who had a huge influence on public opinion. The two of them together must have appeared to be an insurmountable challenge. And everything Hearst and Pulitzer had, the newsboys lacked. The boys were poor, had no influence, and were not particularly well liked by the general population, who considered them little better than dirty street urchins, pestering them to buy papers. That such seemingly powerless kids could force these newspaper moguls to change their ways is a clear testament to the power of activism.

Teens are leading equally impressive activist campaigns today. Here is a look at a few kids who are making a big difference.

The New York newsboys strike of 1899 is an early example of successful youth activism.

Rob Stephens, a nineteen-year-old from North Carolina, became an HIV/AIDS activist after his family adopted a boy and a girl from Kenya, Africa. His new brother had been orphaned after his biological parents died from AIDS-related causes. Stephens, whose family spent time in Africa as missionaries, volunteered in an African orphanage when he was seventeen years old. There he saw the effects the AIDS crisis was having on families. "Orphans weren't a problem before, because the community took them in," he told *Voice of America*, noting that the 13 million AIDS orphans in sub-Saharan Africa have overwhelmed these social structures. "What it creates is an entire society of really old people, and a bunch of kids." He returned to North Carolina and started speaking at schools about the epidemic. He organized a charity basketball tournament. He sold beads made by women in Nairobi. He has led a group of teachers and students to Kenya to visit an African orphanage. Stephens has watched how helping others has changed his fellow students. "It's been phenomenal how this has kind of transformed students' lives. And maybe they won't work on AIDS, but they're more globally aware, and they're more excited about life and hopeful."

Jessie Mehrhoff, a sixteen-year-old in Connecticut, formed Green Teens USA with two high school friends. Green Teens USA teaches about the environment through community projects and education. The group's latest venture is the Compost Caf, which seeks to turn their high school cafeteria into a compost production center. In one year they hope to have their cafeteria produce almost zero waste. They are working on getting rid of all plastic utensils and styrofoam, setting up a composting station behind the school, and getting the school to start using metal utensils and biodegradable plates and trays. Mehrhoff has this advice for would-be activists: "Talk to your friends and get a group of them to support you." As she told *Teen Voices* about recruiting her own friends: "Once we got them excited about what we were doing and all of the positive changes we were making, they were more willing to help us. If you get a small group of people to support you, and then get them to spread the message, I think you'd be surprised at how fast it snowballs, and eventually, you can get your entire school behind you. From there, it can spread to the community."

Ben Byrom, a thirteen-year-old from San Diego, California, helped on the Yes on Prop 2 campaign. Proposition 2, or Prop 2, was a measure that would provide farm animals with more room to move around. In 2008, due to efforts of activists like Byrom, Prop 2 passed in California. Byrom helped on the campaign by gathering signatures, working on mailings, passing out flyers, and sitting in booths at festivals. He even spoke to his social studies class about the issue. Because he has been outspoken, Byrom has faced some criticism but has learned how to deal with it. "When I've been talking to people about Prop 2, lots of them have opposing opinions, and they can be really mean about it," he told Humane Teen. "I usually try to be really polite and engage them in a friendly debate when it comes to animal rights."

All over the world there are teens making a difference in thousands of different ways. There is nothing particularly special about them. They did not need any special background or training. They were just kids who saw something that could be improved and decided to do something about it.

Authors in this anthology examine activism from a variety of perspectives. In addition, the volume contains several appendixes to help the reader understand and explore the topic, including a thorough bibliography and a list of organizations to contact for further information. The appendix titled "What You Should Know About Activism" offers vital facts about activism and how it affects young people. The appendix "What You Should Do About Activism" offers information for young people interested in this issue. With all these features, *Issues That Concern You: Activism* is an excellent resource on this important topic.

ONE

Rules for Activism

Angela Bischoff and Tooker Gomberg

In the following selection Angela Bischoff and Tooker Gomberg offer advice to budding activists on effective activism, or what they call their "Ten Commandments For Changing the World." They provide tips ranging from those that might seem obvious—such as making sure that you are passionate about your cause—to those that are less so, such as making sure that you and others in your group stay healthy and get proper nutrition and exercise. Bischoff has worked with her partner Gomberg on various environmental issues in Canada and around the world. After Gomberg's death Bischoff became an activist on mental health issues.

Changing the world is a blast. It's all the more achievable if you have some basic skills, and lots of chutzpah. With apologies to Moses, and God, here are our top Ten Commandments For Changing the World. Try them out on your issue. Have fun!

But first, some inspiration from [noted linguist and political activist] Noam Chomsky: "If you go to one demonstration and then go home, that's something, but the people in power can live with that. What they can't live with is sustained pressure that keeps building, organizations that keep doing things, people that

Angela Bischoff and Tooker Gomberg, "Ten Commandments For Changing the World," *The ACTivist* magazine, April 17, 2004. Reproduced by permission of the author.

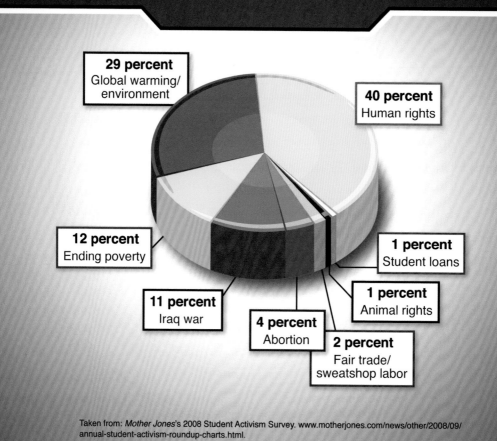

29 percent Global warming/environment

40 percent Human rights

12 percent Ending poverty

1 percent Student loans

11 percent Iraq war

4 percent Abortion

1 percent Animal rights

2 percent Fair trade/sweatshop labor

Taken from: *Mother Jones*'s 2008 Student Activism Survey. www.motherjones.com/news/other/2008/09/annual-student-activism-roundup-charts.html.

keep learning lessons from the last time and doing it better the next time."

The First Steps

1. *You Gotta Believe*. Have hope, passion and confidence that valuable change can and does happen because individuals take bold initiative.

2. *Challenge Authority*. Don't be afraid to question authority. Authority should be earned, not appointed. The "experts" are often proven wrong (they used to believe that the earth was flat!).

You don't have to be an expert to have a valuable opinion or to speak out on an issue.

3. *Know the System.* The system perpetuates itself. Use the tools you have—the telephone is the most underrated. The internet can be of great value for research as well. Learn how decisions are made. How is the bureaucracy structured? Who are the key players? What do they look like? Where do they eat lunch? Go there and talk with them. Get to know their executive assistants. Attend public meetings.

4. *Take Action.* Do something—anything is better than nothing. Bounce your idea around with friends, and then act. Start small, but think big. Organize public events. Distribute handbills. Involve youth. It's easier to ask for forgiveness after the fact rather than to ask for permission. Just do it! Be flexible. Roll with the punches and allow yourself to change tactics mid-stream. Think laterally. Don't get hung-up on money matters; some of the best actions have no budget.

Getting the Word Out

5. *Use the media.* Letters to the Editor of your local newspaper are read by thousands. Stage a dramatic event and invite the media—they love an event that gives them an interesting angle or good photo. Bypass the mainstream media with email and the world wide web to get the word out about your issue and to network.

6. *Build Alliances.* Seek out your common allies such as other community associations, seniors, youth groups, labor, businesses, etc. and work with them to establish support. The system wins through Divide and Conquer, so do the opposite! Network ideas, expertise and issues through email lists. Celebrate your successes with others.

7. *Apply Constant Pressure.* Persevere—it drives those in power crazy. Be as creative as possible in getting your perspective heard. Use the media, phone your politicians, send letters and faxes with graphics and images. Be concise. Bend the Administration's

ear when you attend public meetings. Take notes. Ask specific questions, and give a deadline for when you expect a response. Stay in their faces.

8. *Teach Alternatives*. Propose and articulate intelligent alternatives to the status quo. Inspire people with well thought out, attractive visions of how things can be better. Use actual examples, what's been tried, where and how it works. Do your homework, get the word out, create visual representations. Be positive and hopeful.

Continue to Assess Your Efforts

9. *Learn From Your Mistakes*. You're gonna make mistakes; we all do. Critique—in a positive way—yourself, the movement, and the

The viewpoint's authors recommend that activists use the media to get their views on issues out to the general public.

opposition. What works, and why? What isn't working? What do people really enjoy doing, and do more of that.

10. *Take Care of Yourself and Each Other*. Maintain balance. Eat well and get regular exercise. Avoid burn-out by delegating tasks, sharing responsibility, and maintaining an open process. Be sensitive to your comrades. Have fun. As much as possible, surround yourself with others (both at work and at play) who share your vision so you can build camaraderie, solidarity and support. Enjoy yourself, and nourish your sense of humour. Remember: you're not alone!

So there you have it. Tools for the Evolution. You can easily join the millions of people around the world working towards ecological health and sustainability just by doing something. With a bit of effort, and some extraordinary luck, a sustainable future may be assured for us and the planet. Go forth and agitate.

TWO

Activism Is a Civic Duty

Ralph Nader

"Our lack of civic motivation is the greatest problem facing the country today," writes Ralph Nader in the following essay. When people do not participate in democracy, they cede their power and give corporate and government leaders more control over their lives, he argues. The only way to stop this "downward slide of justice in our society," writes Nader, is for individuals to become activists. Small efforts by many committed activists can make a big difference, he notes, pointing to the success of activists in the United States who managed to accomplish huge change, such as getting women the right to vote, abolishing slavery, and organizing workers. Nader is a noted activist for consumer and public rights. He founded the group Public Citizen, which works for political reform and consumer safety.

"Freedom is participation in power," said the Roman orator Cicero. By this deep definition, freedom is in short supply for tens of millions of Americans, a scarcity with serious consequences. This absence of freedom breeds apathy [a lack of interest]. Average citizens do not fight for change, even about the conditions and causes that mean the most to them.

Ralph Nader, "A Participation in Power," The Nader Page, October 15, 2004. Reproduced by permission.

Our lack of civic motivation is the greatest problem facing the country today. Our beloved country is being taken apart by large multinational commercial powers. Over two thousand years ago, in ancient Athens, a fledgling democracy challenged the long-standing plutocracy [government by the wealthy], using politics as its instrument. The struggle between these two forms of government, one tending to place more power with the people and the other, concentrating power in a few, self-perpetuating hands has been going on under various guises and disguises ever since.

Democracy, whether representative or more direct, brings out the best in people because it gives them more freedom, more voice, more lawful order, and more opportunity to advance their visions of a just society.

In our country, however, there is a gap that needs to be closed: the democracy gap. It is often said that "power abhors a vacuum." When people do not claim power, the greedy step in to fill the void. Every day that capable citizens abstain from civic engagement allows our society and world to tolerate harm and to decay incrementally. The converse is also true. The tiny, cumulative efforts to build a more just society are comparable to the sources for a great river. Similarly, our efforts, small and large, daily and cumulatively, spread the more noble sentiments of our humanity toward one another. But it isn't happening nearly enough to stem the downward slide of justice in our society.

Do Not Give Power to the "Moneyed Interests"

Is it not time for real people to plan for their own futures together? The balance struck between democracy and plutocracy, between fair and unfair tax and budget priorities, between investor rights and corporate managers, between "a government of the people, by the people and for the people," in [Abraham] Lincoln's immortal words, and a government of the Exxons, by the General Motors, and for the DuPonts, determines the quality of our society. It is not coincidental that many centuries ago all the world's great religions cautioned their adherents not to give too much power and position to mercantile interests. So too, our greatest presidents issued warning after warning about "moneyed interests." Franklin Delano Roosevelt emphasized this in a message to Congress, "The liberty of a democracy is not safe if the people tolerate the growth of private power to a point where it becomes stronger than the democratic state itself.

"That in its essence is fascism: ownership of the government by an individual, by a group or any controlling private power." We would do well to heed this age-old wisdom as we ponder why our corporate and political leaders assume more and more control over our lives and futures.

Longtime activist and former presidential candidate Ralph Nader believes it is the civic duty of every American to participate in democracy.

This loss of control is felt ever more deeply. A *Business Week* poll in the year 2000 found 72 percent of the people believing that corporations had too much control over their lives. This was before exposure of the ongoing corporate crime wave that has looted or drained trillions of dollars from hardworking people. Our leaders have been delivering for themselves and their circles, not for the people they allegedly serve.

Giving Up Guarantees Failure

In return, too many people have been too trusting of or too resigned to their leaders' mass media rhetoric. Our static political system often leads our elected officials to do the opposite of what they say. Double talk. With limited choices, people find it difficult to demand more from their leaders, or to have effective modes of measuring their performance beyond the blizzard of soothing words directed at them.

Contemplating participation in power in most contexts, environmental, political, social, economic, technological, invites anxiety. Yet, to throw up one's hands in defeat guarantees anguish and deprivation. Individual obligations absorb daily time and attention, of course, but ignoring our civic obligations, our public citizen duties, profoundly affects our daily lives as well. Most people have developed their own rationalization for not entering civil society as an engaged citizen, such as lack of time or know-how, or concern about slander or retaliation.

A lack of a critical mass of involved citizens on any issue, whatever the scale, contributes to the "see, you can't get anything done," "what's the use," "que sera, sera" [what will be, will be] syndrome which feeds on its own futility. So then, what builds civic motivation? A sense of the heroic progress against great odds achieved by our forebears helps. Think what stamina and inner-strength drove abolitionists against slavery, women seeking the right to vote, workers demanding trade unions to counter the callous bosses of industry, dirt-poor farmers of the late 1800s who, taking on the major railroads and banks, used

Groups Seen as Having Too Much or Too Little Power and Influence in Washington, D.C.

Group	Too Much	Too Little	About Right	Not Sure/ Refused
	Percentage			
Political action committees that give money to political candidates	85	11	3	2
Big companies	84	11	3	2
Political lobbyists	79	14	3	4
The news media	71	20	7	2
TV and radio talk shows	54	31	11	4
Trade associations	52	28	9	11
Labor unions	47	42	7	4
Churches and religious groups	38	51	8	2
Opinion polls	38	49	8	4
Racial minorities	32	54	8	5
Nonprofit organizations	18	68	9	5
Public opinion	17	74	7	2
Small business	6	90	3	1

Note: Percentages may not add up exactly to 100 due to rounding.

Taken from: The Harris Poll, March 7, 2007.

their heads, hearts, and feet to launch the populist-progressive reform movement. These efforts advanced our country immeasurably. They were efforts by ordinary people doing extraordinary things without electricity, motor vehicles, telephones, faxes, or e-mail. They mobilized person-to-person.

People Need to Be Knowledgeable About Their Government

What the citizenry should expect of their governments depends in no small part on how much people know about their governments, their duties, their commitments, and who has unworthy or craven influence over them. There is no substitute for voters doing their homework, studying records, and seeing through the dense mists of fabricated political advertisements, shams, and evasions. Without such civic engagement, and without candidates for office who faithfully represent their constituents, our broken politics cannot be repaired. Whether we think in terms of justice under law or equal protection of the laws, it is untenable [indefensible] that artificial entities called corporations are given most of the constitutional rights of real humans while aggregating powers, privileges, and immunities that individuals, no matter how wealthy, could never come close to attaining.

The primacy of civic values, rooted in our Declaration of Independence and the Constitution, must become our common objective for the common good. When state governments started chartering corporations in the early 1800s, these relatively small business entities were not supposed to be our masters. No one contemplated the emergence of gigantic global conglomerates using governments and trade agreements for their narrow ends. Corporations were seen as our servants under the vigilant rule of law. That's a vision we need to re-create. The people must stand tall so as to reclaim their sovereignty over big business. Strengthening the blessings of liberty and the benefits of justice invites us all to these challenges, both inside the electoral arenas and outside in the civic action arenas.

THREE

Provocative Activism Tactics Work

Jan Frel

In the following selection writer Jan Frel visits the offices of People for the Ethical Treatment of Animals (PETA) to study how, with a relatively small budget, they manage to get so much media attention. He discovers that in PETA's view, any media attention is good, even if it is from someone disparaging PETA. After all, even negative attention raises the issue of animal rights. Frel came away from the experience convinced that this "anything at all" approach works. "How rare to see a non-profit group beating our commercial society at its own game," writes Frel. Frel has been a senior editor for AlterNet.org, TomPaine.com, and the Personal Democracy Forum.

For the record, I am neither a vegan nor a vegetarian. Nor am I an honorary member of People for the Ethical Treatment of Animals (PETA). One of my best friends is, however, and he works at the PETA headquarters in the decrepit asphalt Venice of Norfolk, Va.

I started following PETA's activities because of my personal connection to it, and as I did, I became engrossed with its media tactics, which, to sum them up would be to say they say and do anything at all to draw attention. It sounds simple and obvious

Jan Frel, "PETA: Whatever It Takes," AlterNet, October 5, 2005. Reproduced by permission.

enough—*anything at all*—but it clearly isn't, or other groups would be following its lead. Other than the ACLU [American Civil Liberties Union], which progressive advocacy group (yes, PETA is progressive) garners a regular share of news coverage across the country on a daily basis? Not a single one.

PETA goes after places, people, events and ideas of social meaning and finds a way to seize the headlines—or create its own. It will do whatever it takes to expose people to its point of view. When PETA asks an agricultural town to change its name from say, Cowtown to Liberated Cowtown, it knows that a bored reporter in the surrounding region will fall for it and write a story about it, and that a bunch of readers sick of stories about septic tanks and cattle prices will fall for the headline. Somewhere in that story will be the sentence: "A PETA representative told the mayor that killing animals is wrong."

With that sentence, PETA scores a victory.

Getting Exposure

So PETA sends vegetarian chefs to Camp Casey [the name given to an encampment of antiwar protesters who in 2005 camped outside the Prairie Chapel Ranch in Crawford, Texas, where President George W. Bush was vacationing]; runs semi-nude pictures of Pamela Anderson with anti-fur captions; and urges the USDA [U.S. Department of Agriculture] not to rebuild animal labs at the Katrina-devastated Louisiana State University. And every time PETA gets mentioned in a story, it's a win for the organization— and some real animals might be saved in the process.

Because the truth is, this animal rights thing is a tarpit. The more people are exposed to it, the less comfortable they are with the concept of animal suffering. That's the premise, anyway, and I think it's true.

PETA does have an activist bent in addition to its propaganda arm—real people doing real things to stop the suffering of specific animals—and it has a record of winning in that regard. But because of the fight it's up against—the ubiquity of animal consumption across America—this thing can only be tackled in degrees by exposure to propaganda about it.

Here's the other thing: PETA doesn't care about its general reputation. PETA is just a vehicle for the animal rights movement, and the staff is fully aware of this, so there's no such thing as bad press, and there's absolute indifference to folks who don't like the group's tactics. *Anything at all* that gets PETA in the headlines is a win for the animals.

From that perspective, the pundits and authors who tangle endlessly with PETA's campaigns end up working as suckers for the cause. Take Kathryn Jean-Lopez, a writer for the conservative *National Review*, who was shocked, appalled by PETA's "Holocaust on Your Plate" campaign. Jean-Lopez fell for it badly, offering sentences to the animal rights movement on a silver platter. Perhaps her best was, "I'm not going to deny that a cattle slaughterhouse isn't disgusting." Her blinders were on so tight she managed to bump right into the *anything at all* approach without seeing it: "PETA issues its own reads of the Koran [the Muslim holy book]. It toys with the Book of Mormon. Few beliefs are spared PETA's offensiveness."

Too true. PETA doesn't care about [Mormon founder] Joseph Smith and his Book of Moroni. It cares about animals.

The freakish volume of activity that spills out of PETA is jaw-dropping. Just follow the goings-on of its website (or any of its dozens of spinoff sites)—it unleashes hordes of powerful propaganda, from press releases and videos to images and investigative reports to photogalleries—*anything at all*, and piles of it. I set up a visit with PETA's headquarters to see how it works.

Anything for the Animals

Norfolk is primarily a shipping and Navy base city laid out over a system of ports, rivers and canals. It's got a nuked-out downtown typical of most American cities with a healthy dose of Southern racial segregation and poverty surrounding it. Thousands of jar-headed Navy boys fill the streets at night, clogging the bars and restaurants (many of which offer vegan cuisine as a result of PETA's local influence). The PETA building sticks out from all this. It sits on a small inlet on the Elizabeth River right by a small bridge heading into downtown. It's a modern, shiny, blue-green, five- or six-story glassy blot with a big, fat PETA logo right at the top. Inside about 180 staffers churn out the cause.

When you're writing a story about an organization, the last person in the world you want to get your information from is a member of the communications staff. But in my case that's exactly who I wanted to talk to. My first interviewee was Colleen O'Brien, PETA's communications manager.

PETA's activist tactics include controversial ad campaigns that draw media attention.

As bluntly as possible, I asked her about PETA's sending vegetarian chefs to Camp Casey [location of antiwar protest begun by Cindy Sheehan, mother of slain soldier Casey Sheehan, after he was killed in the Iraq war] in Crawford, Texas during [George W.] Bush's August [2005] vacation: Do you feel like you made a good return on that investment? After all, PETA is not Morgan Stanley; while it's a $25 million a year operation, it still has to pick its battles.

O'Brien started by spinning me, saying, "Vegetarianism is a cruel-free way of living." She said PETA went into Camp Casey with a non-partisan agenda—"Those folks were out there, hungry"—and gave them a vegetarian alternative to eating "decomposing corpses." After I let her go on with this for a while (and yes, putting her quotes in this article is a successful advancement of the animal rights agenda), I tried to bring her back to the issue of whether PETA had mercilessly seized on the fact that hundreds of bored reporters were in Camp Casey, looking to add color to their stories about a poor mother who lost her son in an awful war.

Then she said what I was looking for: "What sets PETA apart from a lot of other groups, is that we have a special relationship with the media. We don't have budgets for the placement of ads like, I suppose, some other groups. We have to do stunts to reach the greatest number of people."

So was the Casey stunt a success? "We had some write-ups," O'Brien said.

Looking back at the coverage from Camp Casey, I found a few mentions. Like the 16th sentence in a Sheehan article from the *Des Moines Register*: "But instead of corn dogs and funnel cakes, they ate veggie burgers grilled by PETA members and free meals cranked out by a volunteer-staffed kitchen." Corn dogs vs. veggie burgers: you couldn't ask for a better contrast for those Iowa readers.

PETA and the Middle East Crisis

I reached back to something for O'Brien that I knew had been a massive publicity success: the fax PETA sent to [Palestinian leader] Yasser Arafat in the spring of 2003 asking him to stop using donkeys as portable bomb devices. A donkey strapped with explosives had recently exploded on the road between Jerusalem and the West Bank settlement of Gush Etzion, killing only the animal.

There's no more dependable source of pious reporting and righteous outrage than the Israeli/Palestinian conflict. And with that letter, PETA struck gold. Network and cable television anchors just couldn't resist a bite on it, including Fox News' Brit Hume (who used the incident as a platform to pop in Ari Fleischer's Orwellification [the use of misleading terms, as in George Orwell's book *Nineteen Eighty-Four*] of the term "suicide bomber"):

> PETA, People for the Ethical Treatment of Animals, has faxed Yasser Arafat protesting the use of a dynamite-laden donkey as a homicide bomber. The group, which complained about the exploding ass but not about the coincidental murder of Israelis, urged Arafat to, quote, "Leave animals out of this conflict."

That's a towering home run for the animal rights movement. A deadpan, [Ronald] Reagan-faced anchor put the Fox watchers on full alert with the mention of Terror, their favorite topic, and also heard a funny pun—dropping their drawbridges to the unconscious wide open. And then an invading direct quote from PETA sprinted right in.

Of course, PETA didn't get anything close to a promise from Arafat, and it didn't really matter. The point is it siphoned piles of headlines and TV coverage away from a bunch of cynical demagogues in the Middle East and in the direction of the animal rights cause. All it took was a fax with an absurd request to the head of the PLO [Palestine Liberation Organization].

I asked Colleen O'Brien if PETA had put out that letter because the organization truly cared about *that* dead donkey or for that matter, donkeys in Palestine. She said it was about that donkey and the donkeys of Palestine, but also the way we think about donkeys in general. She more or less agreed that while the letters, stunts and investigations were contextually about instances of animal suffering, they were more about the soft sell to change mass behavior. Not *that* leather jacket or evil clothing factory, rather the existence of leather jackets, evil clothing factories and the whole clothing market for that matter.

I pressed on with my big Lightning Strikes question: "It's *Anything At All*, isn't it?" Anything at all to get coverage, so that humans stop making animals suffer; any propaganda, any picture, song, performance, that makes an impact. *Anything*, right?

I wish she had said, "Yes. Anything." But I did get a nod in the affirmative. "Look, we're living in a time when the media is titillating," O'Brien said. "If we could sit down with CNN with an investigation, we would. But the reality is that it's not like that. It's a tabloid media." Her hope was to provide "images that stay in people's heads."

Behind the Scenes

After O'Brien left the conference room, I looked out the windows facing the main office. Dozens of PETA staffers sat in a large room, earnestly staring at their computer screens. Handbills and stickers from past campaigns covered the walls, desks and hard drives. One staffer's "companion animal" sat in the aisle with its tail wagging in pure bliss. A mock-up poster of Wendy from Wendy's [fast-food restaurant chain] looked on approvingly, her cleaver fresh and dripping from her latest bovine carve-up session.

Next to speak with me was "Karin Robertson," manager of PETA's Fish Empathy Project. There are quotations around "Karin" because her real name is GoVeg.com. She had it legally changed from Karin Robertson back in 2003, a move that produced piles and piles of headlines (and now a mention here). It still gets a mention pretty much anytime GoVeg's Fish Empathy Project gets in the news.

After we talked about the horrors of the way fish are treated and how they have feelings etc., we came to GoVeg's approach to dealing with the media. GoVeg told me that it's almost impossible to get the press to deal with an issue directly. "They only come up with as many sound bites as possible." I agreed.

"That's why," she said, "we work really hard to make a concise point." A high-vitamin-content sound bite. That's what happened with Brit Hume and the exploding ass, and it's also what happened with GoVeg's project to get the Long Beach California aquarium to stop serving fish.

The sound bites PETA constructs have metrical rules as tight as a haiku. And they must draw on the essential tools of rhetoric—metaphors, powerful images, etc.—or fail; everything has to be in that sound bite or else the soft sell is a failure. GoVeg's sound bite in this case hoodwinked poor Amanda Covarrubias at *The L.A. [Los Angeles] Times*, who put it in the first sentence of her article: "An animal rights group wants the Aquarium of the Pacific in Long Beach to gut its cafeteria menu of fish and seafood, arguing that 'serving fish at an aquarium is like serving poodle burgers at a dog show.'"

At least a dozen other major media outlets ran with that quote, including *The New York Times* and, of course, Fox News.

GoVeg took me on a tour of the rest of the building. There was a room for the Writers Group—a bunch of staffers whose duties

Public Opinion on Animal Rights

May 8–11, 2008 (sorted by "total support")	Support	Oppose
	Percentage	
Passing strict laws concerning the treatment of farm animals	64	33
Banning all product testing on laboratory animals	39	59
Banning sports that involve competition between animals, such as horse racing or dog racing	38	59
Banning all medical research on laboratory animals	35	64
Banning all types of hunting	21	77

Taken from: Gallup Poll, May 8–11, 2008.
http://media.gallup.com/poll/graphs/051508TreatmentofAnimals4_defgxa02ts.gif.

include writing letters to the editor and coordinating volunteers to do the same. She pointed outside to the dog park that's open for the local community to use. The park, of course, sports a message board with plenty of animal rights information for visitors to read.

We also saw the stockroom, where five staffers were busily filling up packets to mail off to PETA's army of volunteer activists.

Using Propaganda

The stockroom was filled with marvelous propaganda covering the full spectrum of *Anything At All*. There were hundreds of small stackable plastic tubs, each with labels like, "306 MOD Caged Chimp Stencil" or "STU 224 Question Authority: PIG." Inside each tub was an exquisite means of communicating the animal rights agenda.

In one drawer I found some wonderful imitations of those 1980s Garbage Pail Kids trading cards. Written in fluid Spanish, they had been designed for Hispanic children. Some caring genius at PETA called the cards *Chupaleches*—"Milk Suckers."

Part of PETA's *Eche La Leche* (Ditch Milk) campaign, the *Chupaleches* on the four-card set I took home feature Ling Ladron De Leche ("Ling the Milk Thief"), a lacto-fattened girl who sports a guilty look on her face as she squats behind the legs of a pissed-off cow and drinks from its udder. The Ling card brilliantly communicates dozens of key things; primarily, that if you tried to get your milk from its true source, you'd find yourself like Ling; eyes averted from the quarry, sucking on the teats of a livid heifer.

The card next to Ling is Andrea Anti-Lactosa, who sits on the toilet clutching her stomach as she deals with the consequences of having poured a whole quart of milk down her gullet. The empty milk container rests at her feet looking like the murder weapon in a crime scene. On the back of Andrea's card is a mockup of a Wanted! notice, which reads: "Blow your nose, it's dripping out! Andrea's got milk, but she also has painful and foul-smelling gas. The faster she quits milk, the faster her family and friends can breathe in peace."

Something a child can understand. . . .

PETA's Success

It was a delight to be in the presence of a winner. How rare to see a non-profit group beating our commercial society at its own game, in aid of something that is truly good for the world. My visit confirmed for me what I had come to believe as a casual observer: PETA is the most successful, iron-fisted, 501c3 [a nonprofit organization] I have ever witnessed; and the only one to make it out of the progressive slums and wage a winning battle at the mass media level.

In tragic contrast to PETA are the scores of non-profits that, despite good faith and hard work, watch their resources sink into the sand, their messages ignored by the public and the media. When I asked Colleen O'Brien why other progressive causes don't adopt PETA's approach, she gave me an absent look. "Their tactics are different from ours. . . . It could be that they are hesitant." That's all I could get out of her.

FOUR

Activist Groups Should Use Less Provocative, More Reasonable Tactics

Shai D. Bronshtein

"Campus activists hold unrealistic goals and use tactics that are poorly designed and alienating to those who might otherwise support them," writes Shai D. Bronshtein of many activist groups at Harvard University. Such groups would be better served, Bronshtein contends, by a more intelligent approach that appeals to people's sense of reason. The author points to a campaign by the campus group Student Labor Action Movement (SLAM) to demand higher wages for janitors. The group had the janitors' children trick-or-treat at the home of the university president to ask for higher wages and benefits for their parents. Bronshtein calls this "completely inappropriate" and a strategy bound to alienate those who might otherwise agree with the group's aims. A far better approach, the author writes, would be for the group to talk to some of Harvard's economists about appropriate wage structures and work from there. Bronshtein is an editorial editor for *The Harvard Crimson*.

Searching for an activist group at Harvard is like going into a substandard ice cream shop. There are far too many flavors, they are all unhealthy, and in the end, they do not even taste good. Across the political spectrum—from the Student Labor Action Movement (SLAM) on the left to Harvard Right to Life (HRL) on the right—campus activists hold unrealistic goals and use tactics that are poorly designed and alienating to those who might otherwise support them. Activists would gain wider acceptance and would be far more effective if they were more reasonable and pragmatic.

The downfall of much campus activism, and what makes it so infuriating and alienating to many, is that rather than appealing to rationality and logic, it appeals to emotions and volatility. A perfect example of this was HRL's series of "Elena" posters [in 2005]. These posters began with a fertilized egg which proudly proclaimed to be Elena, excited to be "alive" and "unique;" but they did not provide real information to the readers other than pointing out that the zygote had chromosomes—much like any other cell.

The posters were meant to be provocative and to cause uneasiness to those who are not certain about when life begins, and HRL proclaimed their campaign a success because it made people think about abortion more critically. Yet while their tactic may have made a small group question their beliefs, it alienated the majority o[n] campus who might be sympathetic to a civil discussion about when life really begins. Very few people argue that abortion would be okay if it was actually killing a person; the debate is deeper and more intricate, and HRL decided simply to incite rather than inform or create dialogue.

Tactics Are Absurd and Alienating

Another example of absurd and alienating tactics from the opposite end of the spectrum was SLAM's stunt of taking janitors' children trick-or-treating at former University President Lawrence H. Summers' home last Halloween [2005] to demand higher wages and increased benefits. Rather than advocating in a professional

Protesters march through Harvard Square in support of pay raises for Harvard's janitors. Some found the students' tactics offensive.

manner, a possibility given the ongoing bargaining between the janitors union and the University, the group decided that the best way to convince Summers that janitors need higher wages was to invade Summers' personal life. This is akin to the students from Social Analysis 10 lobbying Professor N. Gregory Mankiw at his home to curve their midterms up. Most would agree that such a move would be completely inappropriate, which is why tactics that aim to make a scene rather than to convey a real argument often backfire. Those who might otherwise believe that workers should receive better benefits thus avoid SLAM due to its alienating strategies.

Some argue that these methods are completely valid, claiming that they "draw attention" to an argument. Yet in doing so they draw more attention to themselves than to the actual issues. Students at Harvard who are passionate enough about an issue to stage a protest would be more effective if they focused their efforts on the intellectual merit of their arguments. Though inducing others to join a cause through rallies and protests may seem the revolutionary, "cool" thing to do—a throwback to the '60s—to Harvard students and administrators it seems patronizing. Lectures, debates, discussions, informational flyers, and even tabling in a dining hall do far more to legitimate a group and inform others.

Beyond using alienating tactics, many campus activist groups simply have aims that are unreasonable. Many students are driven away to other, more pragmatic causes where they can expect to actually [e]ffect change.

Goals Are Unreasonable

SLAM's "living wage" campaign once again is a prime example. Instead of academically engaging the notion of a living wage and trying to validate it, SLAM ignores the vast literature critical of the notion of a living wage. Instead of talking to Harvard's famed labor economists about how wage structures work, they denounce capitalists. Instead, they work backwards to determine that the "living wage" of a single adult with two children in Boston is $29.64 per hour, an annual income of $62,589, which is about 135% higher than the median household income in the U.S. Boston on a whole has slightly higher wages—the median was $52,792 per year in the 2000 census for the metropolitan area—but whatever benchmark is used, SLAM's figure is inflated. While many on campus agree that Harvard ought to value its workers, it is absurd to claim that Harvard must pay far above the market wage. Because of its unwavering commitment to these ridiculous demands, SLAM drives moderate sympathizers away.

Of course, many campus groups do work for noble causes effectively both at Harvard and in the world at large. They focus on inclusion and the spread of information. They organize letter writing campaigns, speak with representatives and leaders, and generally try to spread information and encourage healthy debate. This is the face that activism should take and often does take in this pragmatic world. People often ask why this generation does not protest, and the answer is that they have found more effective ways to induce change.

Where Does the Future of Activism Stand?

Nowhere
7

Farmers market
38

Facebook
49

The marketplace
50

Congress
56

Campus
63

Percentage

Taken from: 2008 *Mother Jones* Student Activism Survey, 2008.

While dancing around with signs and chanting slogans such as "Harvard you've got cash, why do you pay your workers trash" certainly creates a scene and publicity, it does not actually change people's minds in the end. Most individuals, especially Harvard students and those who consider themselves thoughtful people, would be more easily convinced by an academic, logical, and reasonable approach to change.

FIVE

Extreme Tactics Are Necessary to Stop Animal Abuse

Stop Cal Vivisection

In the following selection members of animal rights activist group Stop Cal Vivisection argue that it is necessary to use extreme tactics to stop animal abuse. In the article the authors graphically describe some of the techniques used on animal testing subjects and argue that, so far, the most effective way to stop such experimentation has been to target the individuals and organizations involved. They note the success of campaigns against researchers who were personally targeted by activists and subsequently abandoned their research. Among the techniques Stop Cal Vivisection recommends are publishing names and addresses of researchers and encouraging activists to contact the researchers to denounce their work. Stop Cal Vivisection is an organization dedicated to ending animal experimentation at the University of California–Berkeley.

In the basement of a large, grey, University of California, Berkeley (UC–Berkeley) building known as the Northwest Animal Facility, 40,000 animals are subjected to the most heinous violence imaginable. And like victims of other forms of oppression, these victims of speciesism [the idea that humans are superior to other animals] are not viewed as living beings capable

Stop Cal Vivisection, "Tortured Consciences Won't Go Away Unless We Make Them," *Earth First! Journal*, 2008. Reproduced by permission.

of thinking, feeling or suffering. They're seen as biomachines. Research subjects. Treated like furry test tubes.

Why are animals being exploited and tortured to death at UC–Berkeley? Because National Institutes of Health grant money makes it a career. Professor Jack Gallant wakes up daily and goes to work, where he locks primates in restraint chairs and deprives them of water. In torment, they're forced to perform visual fixations with electrodes inserted deep into their brains. Yang Dan and Ralph Freeman drive to the building where cats and kittens suffer in stereotaxic [a brain-mapping technique] devices with electrodes inserted into their brains. From birth until death, mechanical stabilization of their eyes restricts them from attaining the smallest of freedoms, even the ability to blink naturally. Frederic Theunissen spends his day drilling holes into the skulls of songbirds bolted into stereotaxic

Cartoon by Mike Flanagan, www.CartoonStock.com.

devices for invasive brain recordings. A conclusion Theunissen has reached after years of his violent studies: "There may exist an overall sexual preference for a male with a sexy song." These are just a few of UC–Berkeley's vivisectors [those who operate on live animals] who have been met over the past year [2008] with a campaign to hold them accountable for the suffering they inflict on sentient beings.

Activist campaigns against vivisection have gained momentum and won victories in recent years. Dario Ringach of the University of California–Los Angeles (UCLA) abandoned vivisection after becoming the target of a campaign. UCLA vivisectors have cops camped out on their lawns to "protect" them from above-ground activists. POM Wonderful abandoned animal testing after becoming the focus of a campaign. Audie Leventhal, formerly of the University of Utah, is no longer torturing non-human primates and has essentially been driven out of state to live in his Nevada vacation home.

Personal Tactics Work

Many of these campaigns have relied on demonstrations that publicly denounce vivisectors at their homes. The Utah House of Representatives passed a bill to conceal the names, personal addresses and phone numbers of University of Utah animal researchers. Activists have been hit with restraining orders in Los Angeles. And on the state level in California, the California Animal Enterprise Protection Act would make it a crime to post the name or address of a vivisector on the Internet.

They're scared because tactics that hit on a personal level work. This is why UC–Berkeley is actively trying to put an end to this sort of resistance with threats of police investigations, media smears and ridiculous rhetoric.

"These people should be banned from harassing people in their homes. They are domestic terrorists, and the FBI has started treating them just as they would al-Qa'ida," UC–Berkeley spokesman Robert Sanders told the *San Jose Mercury News*, referring to the legal, above-ground campaign of Stop

Animal rights activists are starting to borrow the tactics of antiabortion demonstrators by confronting researchers at their homes.

Cal Vivisection. UC–Berkeley effected a removal of Stop Cal Vivisection's website, and sent letters threatening a lawsuit to their new site host, demanding that the "Meet the Vivisectors" page and information about a new lab be removed. Restraining orders have also been threatened, but in recent corporate media coverage, UC–Berkeley admitted that they do not have enough evidence to move forward. The threats to the site host are just as likely only a scare tactic, as all of the information published is legal and could be found in the phone book or with an Internet search.

Last October [2007], 20 activists were arrested in relation to the campaign, but the district attorney never moved forward with charges. There has also been small-scale police repression and spying, as well as sensational quotes about the campaign from the local FBI, but the fight continues. Home demonstrations against vivisectors and others complicit in torture have been occurring frequently.

Contact Those Responsible

A new torture facility is currently being constructed at UC–Berkeley. The $266-million Li Ka-Shing Center for Biomedical and Health Sciences, which is scheduled for completion in March 2010, will include a basement-level vivisection laboratory, and would expand UC–Berkeley's existing Northwest Animal Facility by 70 percent.

To stand a chance at preventing these horrors, we must continue to personalize this struggle. The individuals at UC–Berkeley Capital Projects, McCarthy Building Contractors, and Drilltech Drilling and Shoring have names and addresses. They make the daily choice to assist in oppression. And we have the power to stop them. The people responsible walk our streets, shop in our stores and live in our communities. Hold them accountable by whatever means you are comfortable with, because the horror needs to end.

SIX

Extreme Animal Rights Advocates Are Terrorists

P. Michael Conn

Extreme animals rights activsts should be called terrorists, argues P. Michael Conn in the following viewpoint. Conn, a researcher at a facility that conducts what he describes as "humane, federally regulated animal research," decries the harassment he and his colleagues have received from animal rights activists. When activists publish photos of researchers' children on their Web sites and send letters containing razors to researchers' homes, he writes, their acts go beyond mere activism and become the criminal acts of a terrorist. Conn is a senior scientist at the Oregon Health and Science University's Oregon National Primate Center. He is also the coauthor of *The Animal Research War*.

Words convey more than concepts; they stir up our feelings and direct our thoughts. Racial and religious epithets have started riots, and calling the police officer who pulls your speeding car over "Sir" is a smart way for you to start the conversation.

Animal rights activists know how important words can be. The Northern California–based organization In Defense of Animals and its founder, Elliot Katz, advocate substituting "companion

P. Michael Conn, "Terrorism in the Name of Animal Rights," *Los Angeles Times*, November 12, 2008. P. Michael Conn is coauthor, with James V. Parker, of "The Animal Research War." He is a senior scientist at the Oregon Health and Science University's Oregon National Primate Center and a professor in the university's School of Medicine.

Cartoon by Grizelda, www.CartoonStock.com.

animal" for "pet" and "animal guardian" for "pet owner" in local ordinances and everyday parlance. The idea is "to elicit responsible treatment of companion animals and end abuse, neglect and abandonment of pets."

Well, OK, it's never right to abuse or neglect animals, but U.S. law already contains vigorously enforced animal welfare statutes that require animals to be fed, sheltered and treated as more than just property. It is legal to toss an old coat in a dumpster, but it is not legal to toss an old dog into one.

So if we already distinguish animals from property, why do we need word changes in public ordinances? Probably because many animal rights activists want more. They want to persuade us that animals deserve nearly equal rights with people. "Rights-holders," of course, couldn't be "enslaved" as pets, nor could they be used in scientific research.

Animals Are Not Coequals of People

I'm a researcher and director of research advocacy at the Oregon Health and Science University, where humane, federally regulated animal research is conducted. I don't believe that animals should be treated as the ethical coequals of people. One way to understand the issue is to carry the underlying logic to its extreme: Would you extend to the surviving family of a rabbit the right to sue the fox that killed it? Should a monkey have the right to sue, or have a lawsuit brought on its behalf against a research lab?

Just as Katz's group and others care what words describe pets, I care what words are used to describe animal rights activists. Some, I believe, deserve to be called "terrorists."

In 2001, when I interviewed for a position at a Florida university, I was publicly and privately harassed, followed, threatened and accused of lying about the fact that my own research didn't use animals. A police officer had to be assigned to protect me. Later, the FBI found my name and address among the papers of a man who was arrested for trespassing at the Oregon Health and Science University, a man whose website described how to make firebombs. I can assure you that I felt terrorized.

Much worse has happened to others. Four of my colleagues have received letters "armed" with razors set to cut the hands of anyone who opened them. In August, scientists at UC [University of California] Santa Cruz and their families survived firebombings, and UCLA [University of California–Los Angeles] researchers have been similarly attacked.

Extremists have even posted pictures of scientists' children on their incendiary websites in order to get the scientists to stop animal research. In some cases, they've succeeded.

Extreme Acts Are Terrorism

Of course, the leaders of a few animal rights organizations decry violence and criminal acts, and even the movement's more shadowy groups often claim that they act on the first principle of protecting human and animal life. But the law increasingly sees the movement's extreme actions for what they are.

When 10 activists were convicted of arsons committed from 1995 to 2001 throughout the West (responsibility for the actions was claimed by the Animal Liberation Front and the Earth Liberation Front), U.S. District Judge Ann Aiken applied "terrorism enhancements" that increased sentences for the defendants.

Animal rights activists demonstrate outside the home of a University of California professor. Some people contend that such activists are using terrorist tactics.

In November 2006, the federal Animal Enterprise Terrorism Act was signed into law by President [George W.] Bush, creating tough penalties for damaging property, making threats and conspiring against zoos, research labs and similar enterprises.

Many on both sides of the issue took note of the use of the "T-word" in the name of the act. The science journal *Nature* bristled. "Calling someone a terrorist is a value judgment," it said in an unsigned editorial. While some "knuckleheaded actions could easily have accidentally hurt someone, [the] ethos was to damage property, never to hurt or kill."

Which brings us back to words. Is "knuckleheaded" really the right description for those who place bombs at researchers' residences or under their cars? Is it the right word for targeting children to press their parents to give up animal research?

The terrorist tag is sticking. Just as laws in West Hollywood, San Jose, San Francisco and other cities now term pets "companion animals," federal law is increasingly viewing those who use violence or intimidate by threat of violence as terrorists.

The extremists in the movement will not and should not be able to shed this label unless they rethink their tactics and strategies.

SEVEN

Activism Should Be Taught in Schools

Denis G. Rancourt

The author of the following piece, college professor Denis G. Rancourt, feels that college offers little more than instruction for students on becoming obedient employees. Activism courses are necessary, he argues, because they teach students how to confront authority and use the democratic process, and they expose students to viewpoints that they will not get in other classes. Rancourt felt so strongly that activism should be taught in schools that he used activist techniques to start his own activism class. Rancourt became an "academic squatter"; that is, instead of teaching the class he was assigned to teach, he instead asked his students if they would like to participate in an activism class/social experiment instead. The students liked the idea, and the ensuing battles with the university to keep the class from being canceled offered Rancourt's students a real-life example of activism. Rancourt is a physics professor and environmental science researcher at the University of Ottawa.

I teach an activism course at the University of Ottawa. Not a course about altruism, volunteerism, charity, international aid or civic duty and building community within the confines of the status quo. But an activism course, about confronting authority

Denis G. Rancourt, "Academic Squatting—a Democratic Method of Curriculum Development," Activist Teacher, April 13, 2007. Reproduced by permission.

and hierarchical structures directly or through defiant or non-subordinate assertion in order to democratize power in the workplace, at school, and in society.

As is often the case with effective activism, this course is itself direct, overt, and defiant. I have chosen to adopt a style consistent with this stance in writing this article, as an illustration of my pedagogical posture. Teachers need to show what they stand for and more and more we need to stand for something beyond doctrinal platitudes.

The underlying working premise of all other courses on my campus is that our societal structures are mostly beneficial and just—that the schools and other private and public institutions, government institutions, corporations, and financial institutions all work together to generate wealth and distribute services and resources. The underlying assumption of all other courses is that societal structures may perhaps need to be adjusted but are necessary in some form and mostly benefit society.

The Premise of the Course

In contrast, the underlying premise of the activism course is that our societal structures, taken together, represent the most formidable instrument of oppression and exploitation ever to occupy the planet—that the reality of these structures is one of continental-scale pillaging enforced by the greatest military and coercion machines ever assembled. In this paradigm, the observed generalized criminal disregard for local inhabitants and indigenous peoples is no accident; the environment, workers and inhabitants are structurally expendable liabilities in a profit-driven debt-based global financial enterprise that must be characterized as insane, not to mention unsustainable; and the schools and universities supply the obedient workers and managers and professionals that adopt and apply this system's doctrine—knowingly or unknowingly, according to need.

This is the outlook that informs the speakers I invite, the readings I suggest, the way I position science and all the disciplines, the way I guide whole class discussions, and the one-on-one interactions I have with students.

Should High Schools Require Community Service?

Yes. Students have a responsibility to give back to their communities, and it is reasonable to require volunteering as a prerequisite for graduation.

61 percent

Maybe. Schools should not make volunteering mandatory, but they should offer ample opportunities for volunteerism, and they should reward students who participate.

31 percent

No. Schools should focus on creating a rigorous academic environment to prepare students for college and beyond, and they should let volunteering be a personal student decision.

7 percent

Taken from: The Edutopia Poll, Edutopia, February 2, 2009. www.edutopia.org/node/5984/results.

I think there should be room for at least one such course on my campus.

The university administration and many of my colleagues do not share my zeal for this diversity of perspective—as has been amply demonstrated and documented over the last few years. Their attacks on the activism course experiment are strong testaments to the uncompromised position and moral and intellectual rigour that the students and I have chosen to apply and defend.

The Beginnings of the Class

It all started with a modest experiment in pedagogy and social relevance in the fall of 2005. In response to twenty years of observing classes that both delivered soulless material and served mainly to prepare students to be obedient and indoctrinated employees, I felt I had to do something more than give a "better" physics course. I realized that it is activists, not obedient employees, who make a difference, who make the world a better place.

I decided that the course would itself be a realization of activism. I decided to squat the Physics and the Environment course that had been assigned to me that fall. This may have been the first example of overt academic squatting, where one openly takes an existing course and does with it something different.

For a squat to succeed, the occupants have to be on board, and at the first class the students embraced the project with more enthusiasm than I could have imagined. I had simply suggested that maybe the greatest societal problems around were as important as physics, that the students themselves could be in charge of their own learning, and that I saw no need for grading or any institutional evaluation.

The experiment encountered immediate and explosive resistance. After the VP-Academic [vice president of academic affairs] choked on the course web site, we were treated to a tantrum from the Dean of Science at the second class. What followed was a textbook example of successful activism, to the point that several students asked if the administration's response had been completely staged, and some thanked the dean for providing a laboratory component to the physics course.

At the third class, the dean was back to announce a negotiated agreement "to the benefit of all" that would have us—the students and I—run the course exactly as we had intended. But we knew the victory would be short lived if we did not get an activism course on the books, and so we fought our way through 11 months and 16 committee meetings to have SCI 1101 approved, as a credited Faculty of Science course with no prerequisites. Despite official recognition of this first multidisciplinary Science (SCI)-code course on our campus, in the words of an enlightened Science Faculty Executive, SCI 1101 "does not count as a science course."

A Phenomenon in the Community

The activism course exists because hundreds of students and community members fought for it against committee normalcy, unprecedented administrative barriers, disciplinal ghettoism, and regressive opinion echoed by the mainstream media. It has received unequalled praise from both its paying "clients" (as the administration calls students) and "freeloading" community participants. Many attest to a life-changing experience, like only discovering one's agency and place in the world can produce.

At the very least, the students of the activism course were exposed to speakers and issues that they did not encounter in other courses, often had their first university encounter with intrinsic motivation, deeply questioned the pedagogical methods of other courses, and often became leading campus activists. In the words of one student: "Everything else is the same but this course is real."

The more activists there are, the more democracy there is.

In contrast and true to character, the university executive has consistently attempted to block the course over the past two years: From the dean's failed in-class intervention, to deflected attempts to censor the course web site, to ad hoc rules and evaluation committees, to forbidding community member participation, to failed disciplinary campaigns based on ridiculous premises, to withholding academic resources, to the upper executives re-writing the course description themselves, and most recently to expelling students on the basis of age.

The opposite atmosphere reigns in the classroom, where hundreds of students of all ages (10 to 70+) and backgrounds interact with intricate and compelling material of direct relevance to their place in the world. Principal actors, experts, and readings present vital issues including: war, terrorism, the armament industry, monetary economics, poverty, professional ethics, environmental issues, societal and institutional structures, human rights, science funding, the non-profit sector, the agri-food industry, the pharmaceutical industry, animal rights, democracy, foreign policy, and others. Self-motivation and unrestrained exploration and expression are enabled by the absence of grades and by individually designed progress reports.

Activism in colleges and universities is demonstrated by including it in the curriculum and by students protesting against issues such as high tuition costs.

Professors Need to Be Activists

Academic squatting works! Academic squatting is needed because universities are dictatorships, devoid of real democracy, run by self-appointed executives who serve private capital interests. Producing obedient employees and publicly funded intellectual property transfers are in fact the university's only business, as is evident from its research, programs, curricula, and coercive methods. Of course, there are accidental side benefits that may be realized by individual students, just as friendships can develop in a labour camp, and one can marry a prison guard one met on the inside, or write a good book while in exile, but the point is that the university is an instrument of power as it has always been, period. Only activism—resistance—can change that.

One antidote to the university as boot camp in the service of capital is for tenured professors to use their tenure. This would turn tenure on its head, as it is free society's coercive tool of choice for fabricating aligned and docile academics. Not the job security in itself, which should be available to all, but the filtering and moulding process known as the tenure track. But why not turn tenure on its head? Tenure is death, risk is life, and collaboration is criminal. Collaborating in an institutionalized system of resource looting, labour exploitation, and genocidal demographic engineering is criminal, especially when its ultimate weapon is the foremost crime known as war, such as the present Canadian war in Afghanistan.

Tenure—use it or lose it.

Alternatively, the next step is academic hijacking, where students tell a professor that she can stay or leave but that this is what they are going to do and these are the speakers they are going to invite. . . . Here, academic freedom would apply to students, not just professors. Now that would be taking responsibility for one's education.

Epilogue: Despite filling the largest auditorium on campus and despite large petitions, student demonstrations and over one hundred letter testimonials from former students, SCI 1101 was never offered again after its inauguration in the fall semester of 2006. I was fired for my dissidence under false pretext on March 31, 2009, in what is considered a major academic freedom case in Canada. I was a Full Professor with tenure and a highly recognized scientific researcher. My case is documented here: http://rancourt .academicfreedom.ca/. This informs us about the present state of academic freedom in Canada.

When student council members tried to discuss the possibility of offering SCI 1101 again and of creating a second year SCI 2101 at the Council of the Faculty of Science, the dean of the faculty violated council by-laws in order to avoid the agenda item. The dean then cancelled council meetings for the next 10 months. When meetings resumed, the dean explained that SCI 1101 would not be offered by any professor because he was worried about "academic hijacking."

—Denis Rancourt, Ottawa, May 2009.

EIGHT

Requiring Activism in Schools Cannot Replace the Real Thing

James Hershberger

> James Hershberger was inspired to write the following piece during college. He had been looking forward to attending two protest rallies at his school until he discovered that the protests had been scheduled as part of a project for two different sections of a history class. "I find something disingenuous about students holding up signs and chanting slogans, not because of a passionate desire for progress, but to earn a good grade," he writes. He found such required activism especially disheartening because it coincided with what he saw as a drop in actual activism at his school. Hershberger wrote this as the opinions editor of *The Daily Toreador*, the student newspaper of Texas Tech University in Lubbock, Texas.

In my book, there's nothing quite as sweet as political protests, except maybe cherry snow cones.

Since I was little, I remember seeing pictures of the women's suffrage parades and Martin Luther King Jr.'s march on Washington D.C., and realizing the honor in standing up against the establishment. I admired those brave enough to demonstrate their opposition to policies and waited for my time to join them.

James Hershberger, "Almost Activism," *Daily Toreador*, April 21, 2006. Reproduced by permission.

I was excited when I heard there would be two protests at Texas Tech [University] this week [April 2006]. One was against people not being able to park on campus after 5:30 p.m. without a parking permit, and the other was against student apathy, both worthy causes that I agree with.

Word was getting around and the spirit of revolution filled the atmosphere. There were some clever fliers by the parking faction that mocked parking tickets being passed around and interesting ideas were being discussed about how to best get the point across. Though as an employee at *The Daily Toreador* I'm supposed to report the news rather than make it, I was looking forward to stopping by the events and encouraging the protesters.

A Class Requirement

However, all my enthusiasm left me when I learned that the protests were part of a project for two different sections of a history class.

Don't get me wrong; I definitely give kudos to the professor for coming up with a creative assignment. I also commend the students for being willing to participate even though some left their comfort zones.

Yet, I find something disingenuous about students holding up signs and chanting slogans, not because of a passionate desire for progress, but to earn a good grade. I found out they chose their cause based on class consensus, not because of glaring injustice. It felt contrived, false. How ironic is it that a protest against apathy had to be spurred by a professor?

Maybe my resentment is misdirected. These students did raise awareness to some important issues and utilitarian philosophy says the ends justify the means. I just find it frustrating that interest in political activism has seemed to be declining at Tech since I came here back in Fall 2002.

"Real" Activism Declining

I remember participating in a protest freshman year about the lack of diversity in Tech's predominately white and male faculty. A stream of more than 100 people marched from the law school

Some are concerned that students involved in college activism classes are motivated by getting a good grade and not by a desire for progress.

to Memorial Circle, singing songs and carrying signs. I remember encountering people I knew from classes staring at me in disbelief as I carried my poster reading "Being diverse is a blessing, not a curse." They asked me about it in the following days, and I was able to share my views with other people on that subject.

In previous years, Tech has held a "Take Back the Night" march, a demonstration against violence. The march would commence in Memorial Circle where a guest speaker, one year it was a rape survivor, would deliver a speech on the need to stop violence. It would close with a candlelight vigil to honor those who lost their lives. No march has been organized for this year.

Different Ways to Encourage Activism

Do you support or oppose the following national service proposals?

	Strongly support	Support/ oppose
Giving college scholarships to people who agree to serve as police officers, firefighters, or in civil defense	40	75/24
Making it possible for people who do not itemize on their tax returns to receive a tax deduction for charitable donations	40	72/23
Requiring all graduating high school students to complete a certain number of hours of community service to receive their diploma	38	62/37
Dramatically enlarging America's national service program	32	70/21
Requiring all eighteen-year-olds to attend a three-month session of basic training for civilian or military service	31	49/48
Instituting a new kind of draft that gives people a choice between civilian or military service	30	60/29

Taken from: "How Americans Feel About Politics After 9/11," Democratic Leadership Council (DLC), December 12, 2001. www.ndol.org/ndol_ci.cfm?contentid=250017&subid=269&kaid=127.

I used to know a lot of student activists who led protests and worked to bring about improvement. These people have graduated, and it seems no one has stepped up to replace them and as a result, the units of political activism have decayed. Lubbock was one of the few large cities in Texas that did not have a protest about Congress' proposed illegal immigration laws, while students in junior high conducted school walk-outs. The faculty at Tech remains as white and male as it was four years ago, but what is lacking is people being mad about it.

The officers of the Student Government Association [SGA] receive salaries ranging from $1,250 for the president to $1,000 for the vice-presidents and $500 for the other three officers, according to a previous *Daily Toreador* article. These officers also have permits to park in the lot in front of the Student Union, a much more convenient location than the commuter lots. I do not feel like my student fees go to good use by paying these salaries when the SGA doesn't do much. I bet many students agree, but again, where is the movement to right this wrong?

Maybe Real Activism Will Follow?

Despite the seemingly dismal situation of these and other concerns going unanswered, I remain hopeful. I know there are students on this campus who are interested in greater things than beer and TV. There are people who are leaders and have courage and want to leave Tech better than they found it. I want to see these people rise up and rattle [the] cages of those who take advantage of ignorance and abuse those who can't speak for themselves like my friends and I used to do. Conjure the spirit of activism again. Get pissed off about the injustice happening on campus and in the world and do something about it.

A pair of history classes reminded us Thursday about the honor of activism by replicating protests. Now let's see the real revolutionaries come forth to stick it to the man. Back in the day, the Tech newspaper's unofficial motto was "raising constructive hell on Texas Tech campus."

Raiders, you have my blessing in your endeavors to raise some constructive hell.

NINE

Teachers Have a Right to Express Political Beliefs in School

Leo Casey

> Leo Casey wrote the following essay in response to a New York City Department of Education announcement during the 2008 presidential election that teachers would not be allowed to wear political buttons or clothing during school or school activities. Casey argues that teachers not only have a right to share political viewpoints, but a duty to do so. "Teachers have a unique and special responsibility in a democracy: we are citizens in our own right, and we are the educators of the next generation of citizens. Properly understood, these two roles are inextricably linked, one to the other," writes Casey. Leo Casey is a teacher and vice president of academic high schools of the United Federation of Teachers in New York City.

As we prepare for our national elections, it is well worth remembering that the highest office in American democracy is not the President, but the citizen. In a democracy, "we the people"—the body of citizens—must rule. Elected officials, including our President, are only our representatives; they exercise the powers we grant to them.

The citizen bears not only rights, but responsibilities. Our vote and our participation in free and fair elections that choose

Leo Casey, "Teaching Democratic Leadership and Freedom of Political Expression," Edwize, October 4, 2008. Reproduced by permission of the author.

our representatives is not simply the greatest power and right of the citizenry, won by Americans who struggled courageously throughout our history to extend the franchise to all, regardless of class, sex and race. Just as importantly, it is our greatest civic responsibility. The strength and resilience, the purpose and ends, of democracy rests upon the active participation of the citizenry in elections: to the extent that government does not have a clear mandate of the citizenry due to widespread abstention from the electoral process, its authority is greatly diminished. That is the import of Thomas Jefferson's and John Locke's famous notion that legitimate government is based on the consent of the governed.

Teachers have a unique and special responsibility in a democracy: we are citizens in our own right, and we are the educators of the next generation of citizens. Properly understood, these two roles are inextricably linked, one to the other. One does not educate youth into democratic citizenship by lecture and dictate. Rather, it is essential that we teachers model good citizenship and that our classrooms embody the fundamental values of free expression, fairness and thoughtful deliberation that define all democratic decision-making, including free elections. Students learn how to be good citizens by actual[ly] practicing the skills of citizenship in the classroom and in the school. In so doing, they develop the capacity to think critically and independently and to engage in dialogue and debate on matters political. In this respect, presidential elections are a special "teachable moment," in which students are unusually motivated and predisposed to engage in the practice of those skills, taking the first steps in critical thought and political debate. At this and other times, a teacher must be a good democratic citizen to be an educator of democratic citizenship.

The First Amendment's guarantee of freedom of political expression and freedom of political association is thus an indispensable foundation of both democratic citizenship and citizenship education in the United States. The will of the people can only be known and exercised when three conditions are met: first, there is a robust and vigorous public debate which presents policy alternatives; second, there is a clear choice between representatives who are pledged to enact those policy alternatives; and third, there is a deliberative process in which the citizenry—as well as the candidates for public office—engage each other. Without freedom of expression and freedom of association, none of this is possible; it is the sine qua non [a prerequisite] of democracy. This is why the Supreme Court has given the broadest protections, among all constitutional rights, to political expression and association. Similarly,

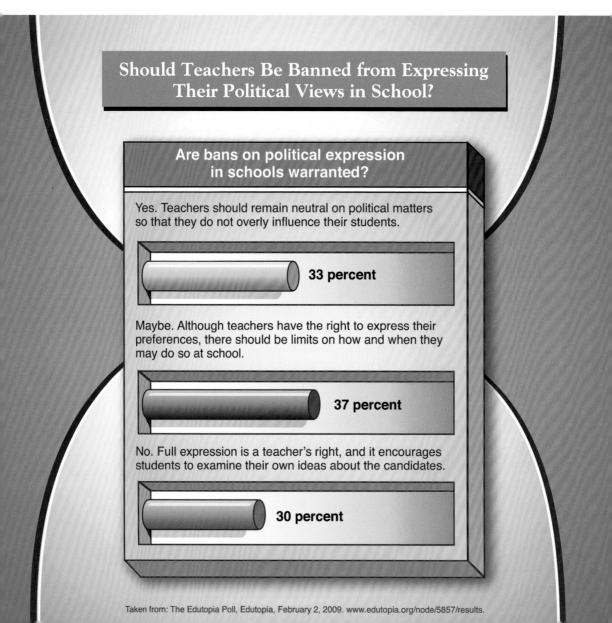

Should Teachers Be Banned from Expressing Their Political Views in School?

Are bans on political expression in schools warranted?

Yes. Teachers should remain neutral on political matters so that they do not overly influence their students.

33 percent

Maybe. Although teachers have the right to express their preferences, there should be limits on how and when they may do so at school.

37 percent

No. Full expression is a teacher's right, and it encourages students to examine their own ideas about the candidates.

30 percent

citizenship education in the classroom demands a foundation of free expression and free inquiry.

The founding slogan of the American Federation of Teachers, "Education for Democracy, Democracy for Education," reflects the preeminent place teacher unionists have always given to democratic citizenship education. We believe that there is a world of difference between such democratic citizenship education and efforts to proselytize students into a particular political or ideological perspective, a practice which we have steadfastly opposed throughout our history. A teacher who engages in political proselytizing, or who treats students differently based on [the] political views they hold, is a teacher who betrays the trust a democratic society has placed in him or her as an educator of the next generation of citizens.

In breaking with at least a quarter century of its own precedent, the [New York City] Department of Education [DoE] announced in this week's P-Weekly [periodic assessments weekly update] that the First Amendment rights of staff to free political expression should be restricted in schools. "School staff may not wear buttons or apparel in support of a political candidate while in school or during school activities," principals were told. Further, "the distribution or posting of materials in support of a political candidate in a school building" was prohibited. For as long as I have taught in New York City public schools, through some six presidential elections, four elections for each Senator and twelve elections of members of the House of Representatives, five gubernatorial elections, five mayoral elections and more state and citywide ballot referenda than I can recall, the Board of Education/Department of Education had a very different policy. There was no prohibition of election campaign buttons, and no attempt was made to prevent the UFT [United Federation of Teachers] from communicating with its members on participation in the electoral process in schools. When educators were at the helm of New York City public schools, they saw no harm, but rather some worthwhile good, in students knowing that their teachers were engaged in the primary right and responsibility of citizenship, participation in the electoral process. Why the DoE chose this moment to establish a new policy limiting free political expression will have to be explained by those who took this

United Federation of Teachers president Randi Weingarten (pictured) has stated that the UFT is willing to go to federal court to defend the right of teachers to exercise free political expression in schools.

unfortunate step, but one thing is clear: those who now occupy Tweed [Courthouse—New York City DoE headquarters] do not understand the fundamental distinction between education into democratic citizenship, modeled by teachers who practice that citizenship, and the inappropriate use of the classroom to proselytize a particular political view or ideology. Their actions can not but have a chilling effect on citizenship education.

It is worth pointing out that, to be consistent here, the DoE would have to prohibit from public schools the numerous newspapers and newsmagazines which do not simply state a preference for this candidate or that political party, as a political button does, but make as convincing a case as they can that their readers should embrace that same choice. Note that it would be the exceptional school which could afford and provide print media on different sides of an election campaign, especially since the editorial choices of the different publications is not always clear at the outset of a campaign. And remember that many a tabloid journal makes little practical distinction between its editorial stance and its news coverage. But if there is a positive educational purpose in having students read and analyze such media advocacy, in learning how to become a critical consumer of such information, why do we need to protect students from the mere knowledge that a teacher is actively supporting a candidate or a cause? If the DoE would not censor print media during an election campaign, why should it censor such modest political expression as a button on the part of educators?

UFT President Randi Weingarten has made clear that if necessary, the UFT will go to federal court to defend the First Amendment rights of school staff to free political expression in schools. What is at stake is not simply the rights of educators, but a vibrant education into democratic citizenship.

TEN

Teachers Should Not Express Political Beliefs in the Classroom

Thomas Sowell

> In the following viewpoint Thomas Sowell argues that teachers are unique in thinking they should be allowed to share their political views as part of their jobs. After all, he writes, a plumber does not expect to include a lecture on foreign policy while working on someone's house. Sowell is an economist, conservative author, and senior fellow of the Hoover Institution at Stanford University.

Governor Bill Owens of Colorado has cut through the cant about "free speech" and come to the defense of a 16-year-old high school student who tape-recorded his geography teacher using class time to rant against President [George W.] Bush and compare him to [Adolf] Hitler.

The teacher's lawyer talks about First Amendment rights to free speech but free speech has never meant speech free of consequences. Even aside from laws against libel or extortion, you can insult your boss or your spouse only at your own risk.

Unfortunately, there is much confusion about both free speech and academic freedom. At too many schools and colleges across the country, teachers feel free to use a captive audience to vent their politics when they are supposed to be teaching geography or math or other subjects.

Thomas Sowell, "Classroom Brainwashing," Real Clear Politics, March 14, 2006. By permission of Thomas Sowell and Creators Syndicate, Inc.

While the public occasionally hears about weird rantings by some teacher or professor, what seldom gets any media attention is the far more pervasive classroom brainwashing by people whose views may not be so extreme, but are no less irrelevant to what they are being paid to teach. Some say teachers should give "both sides"—but they should give neither side if it is off the subject.

Colorado governor Bill Owens stirred controversy when he came to the defense of a student who tape-recorded a teacher expressing political views in class.

Academic freedom is the freedom to do academic things—teach chemistry or accounting the way you think chemistry or accounting should be taught. It is also freedom to engage in the political activities of other citizens—on their own time, outside the classroom—without being fired.

Nowhere else do people think that it is OK to engage in politics instead of doing the job for which they are being paid. When you hire a plumber to fix a leak, you don't want to find your home being flooded while he whiles away the hours talking about Congressional elections or foreign policy.

Teachers Are Not Paid to Spout Political Opinions

It doesn't matter whether his political opinions are good, bad, or indifferent if he is being paid to do a different job.

Only among "educators" is there such confusion that merely exposing what they are doing behind the backs of parents and taxpayers is regarded as a violation of their rights. Tenure is apparently supposed to confer carte blanche [complete authority to act as one chooses].

The Colorado geography teacher is not unique. A professor at UCLA [University of California–Los Angeles] wrote an indignant article in the *Chronicle of Higher Education*, denouncing organized efforts of students to record lectures of professors who impose their politics in class instead of teaching the subject they were hired to teach.

All across the country, from the elementary schools to the universities, students report being propagandized. That the propaganda is almost invariably from the political left is secondary. The fact that it is political propaganda instead of the subject matter of the class is what is crucial.

The lopsided imbalance among college professors in their political parties is a symptom of the problem, rather than the fundamental problem itself.

If physicists taught physics and economists taught economics, what they did on their own time politically would be no more relevant than whether they go swimming or sky diving on their days off. But politics is intruded, not only into the classroom, but into hiring decisions as well.

American Professors and Politcal Party Affiliation

Party Affiliation	Percentage
Strong Democrat	32.4
Weak Democrat	18.6
Independent/Democrat	19.8
Independent	8.5
Independent/Republican	7.0
Weak Republican	8.7
Strong Republican	5.0

Taken from: Neil Gross and Solon Simmons, "The Social and Political Views of American Professors," Harvard University, September 24, 2007.

Even top scholars who are conservatives are unlikely to be hired by many colleges and universities. Similarly with people training to become public school teachers. Some in schools of education have said that, to be qualified, you have to see teaching as a means of social change—meaning change in a leftward direction.

Such attitudes lead to lopsided politics among professors. At Stanford University, for example, the faculty includes 275 registered Democrats and 36 registered Republicans.

Such ratios are not uncommon at other universities—despite all the rhetoric about "diversity." Only physical diversity seems to matter.

Inbred ideological narrowness shows up, not only in hiring and teaching, but also in restrictive campus speech codes for students, created by the very academics who complain loudly when their own "free speech" is challenged.

So long as voters, taxpayers, university trustees, and parents tolerate all this, so long it will continue.

ELEVEN

Celebrity Activists Can Draw Attention to Causes

Peter Ford and Gloria Goodale

In the following viewpoint Peter Ford and Gloria Goodale discuss the trend of celebrity activism and celebrities' motivation. According to the article, while some celebrities donate time and money because they believe in a cause, others do it simply because it is the "in" thing. However, Ford and Goodale willingly admit that most agencies need a celebrity endorsement in order to help raise awareness for their causes. Peter Ford and Gloria Goodale are both staff writers and regular contributors to *The Christian Science Monitor*.

When Formula One world champion Michael Schumacher decided to contribute $10 million to tsunami-relief efforts [in 2005], he did not hide his light under a bushel.

Instead, the race-car driver had his manager announce the gift in a phone call to a nationally broadcast telethon in his native Germany. As the largest known individual donation, the gesture drew instant global attention.

So did Sandra "Miss Congeniality" Bullock's gift of $1 million to the American Red Cross, Steven Spielberg's donation of $1.5 million to several charities, and Leonardo DiCaprio's "sizable" contribution to the United Nations Children's Fund (UNICEF).

Motivation for Charity

They raised a few eyebrows, too, among observers who are trying hard not to be cynical, but wonder whether the international outpouring of celebrity generosity in the wake of the Asian tsunamis might sometimes be motivated as much by self-promotion as by philanthropy.

The film stars, musicians, and athletes who have publicly pitched in to pay for disaster relief are caught "in a dialectic of aggrandizement and responsibility," says Paul Schervish, head of the Center on Wealth and Philanthropy at Boston College. "If helping others is in your strategic self-interest as a signal of who you are . . . that can be read cynically or non-cynically."

Mr. Schumacher, of course, like other big-name givers, could have avoided raising any doubts by making their donations anonymously.

But that would have missed an opportunity, says Schumacher's spokeswoman, Sabine Kehm. "He wanted others to be encouraged by his donation," she explains. "He felt it would be good if people saw others were doing something, which would invite them to do something too."

It worked, Ms. Kehm insists. The telethon to which Schumacher pledged his money raised 40 million euros ($53 million)—four times the amount collected by a similar television drive a night earlier.

"Because our society . . . deifies our celebrities, we expect them to somehow become our role models," suggests Marc Pollick, who heads The Giving Back Fund, which advises celebrities about charity. "Celebrities have the dual assets in our culture of wealth and fame. If they choose, they can leverage both on behalf of whatever cause they believe in."

The Trend of Celebrity Activism

Stars of every stripe have been doing their bit for tsunami victims over the past two weeks [in January 2005]. The rock band Linkin Park seeded an organization dubbed "Music for Relief" with $100,000. Chinese singers have staged marathon benefit concerts. Four-time world heavyweight boxing champion Evander

Celebrities and Their Causes

Bono	Debt AIDS Trade Africa (DATA)
Sandra Bullock	American Red Cross
Nicholas Cage	Homelessness, Hurricane Katrina Relief
Jackie Chan	Hong Kong Youth, UNICEF
Celine Dion	Canadian Cystic Fibrosis Foundation
Angelina Jolie	The United Nations Refugee Agency
Oprah Winfrey	The Oprah Winfrey Foundation

Taken from: "Generous Celebs," *Forbes*, May 4, 2006.
www.forbes.com/2006/05/04/cx_me_0505featslide.html?thisSpeed=30000.

Holyfield visited Sri Lanka with a disaster-relief team. In Britain, Princes Harry and William packed supplies destined for Asia.

Celebrities now appear almost obliged to be seen to care. In today's celebrity-driven culture "the closer these people get to the gods, the more they feel they have to give something back," says Maria Zanca, head of celebrity relations for UNICEF.

At the same time, says Mario Almonte, vice president of the Herman Associates public relations firm in New York, celebrities "tend to be followers of trends. They want to be with the 'in' crowd. They go to the 'in' restaurants. They donate to the 'in' charity."

The trend of celebrity association with good causes began with Danny Kaye, UNICEF's first goodwill ambassador, who toured the world on the agency's behalf in 1954.

Over the decades, a number of other famous names have worn their hearts on their sleeves. [Former Beatle] George Harrison organized a concert for Bangladesh in 1971; [singer-songwriter] Bob Geldof raised huge sums for Ethiopian famine victims with Band Aid in 1984; five supermodels appeared together nude on posters proclaiming they would "rather go naked than wear fur"; U2's Bono spends as much time campaigning for Third-World causes as he does singing.

Their fame gives celebrities an advantage in promoting their causes, as when rock singer Bono met with President George W. Bush about providing aid to African nations battling HIV epidemics.

Charities Need Celebrities to Raise Awareness

Today, most aid agencies find that they need a star or two to help them make their case, and to bring their cause to the forefront of public attention.

The 30 or so celebrities who boost UNICEF, including Nicole Kidman and David Beckham, "are of huge value," says Ms. Zanca. "They give a face and voice to all those people with no faces and no voices. When a celebrity talks, people listen; there is no better messenger."

Phil Bloomer, head of advocacy for Oxfam UK, agrees. "They can reach into people's lives and speak to them in ways that Oxfam spokesmen cannot," he says. "They can reach out to people who might not normally listen to what Oxfam has to say."

This works—for the star and for the aid group—only if the celebrity is sincere and clearly cares, says Mr. Pollick. Being publicly philanthropic "takes a sincerity and authenticity," he cautions. "Anything not done for the right reasons will soon become apparent to the public."

When things go wrong with stars they can be "horrendously embarrassing," says one development expert. "For a good number of celebrities there is a marketing opportunity in all this. All they want is a photo-opportunity with a poor African kid."

That was not the case with Princess Diana, whose effort against landmines "set the stage for the modern conjunction of celebrity and public causes," says Thomas Goodnight, who teaches a course in celebrity advocacy at the University of California in Los Angeles.

Many aid workers are happy to accept a "quid pro quo" in their relationships with stars. "If they get as much out of it as we do, so long as we don't think that is the main reason they are doing it, why should I be bothered?" asks Zanca.

In the end, adds Toby Miller, who teaches film at the University of California, "what matters is the quality and the quantity of the giving . . . the good done on the ground, much more than any motivation."

TWELVE

Celebrity Activists Divert Attention from the Real Issues

Ross Clark

> In the following selection Ross Clark discusses celebrities and their use of charities as a way to self-promote. According to the article, celebrities tend to jump on a charity bandwagon and follow the trend of giving as a way to revive their careers and draw attention to them, instead of focusing on the issues at hand. Ross Clark is a freelance journalist and frequent columnist for *The Spectator*.

It was not until the first week of January [2005] that the full tragedy of the Asian tsunami became clear. Millions of Britons had whipped out their credit cards from their pockets, gone online and donated tens of millions of pounds—directly to charities which were working in South Asia. They hadn't had the decency to wait to buy the charity single, sung by Paul Weller, or to pause until 'Radio Aid' day on 17 January and phone their donations into [presenters] Chris Evans, Zoe Ball and their special guest, [British prime minister] Tony Blair. They didn't even save their cash for the chance to buy [actors] Liam Neeson's Armani tuxedo or Kate Winslet's ball-gown in an online charity auction, or to head to see [musical artists] Lulu and Eric Clapton at Tsunami Relief Cardiff in the Millennium Stadium. No, Sid and Doris from Nuneaton, the buggers, just went ahead and gave the money straight to charities working with the victims, bypassing the celebrity industry altogether.

It is hard to put into words the suffering this has caused. Imagine you are a washed-up 1980s pop star trying to revive your career or a C-list celeb trying to make the big time. And before you've had a chance to get your name on the bill of some charity ball, the likes of Médecins Sans Frontières are putting it about that actually they've got quite enough money for the first stage of their tsunami relief operation, thank you very much, but would you please keep us in mind for the next disaster? It doesn't bear thinking about: the sense of helplessness, of worthlessness which must be felt by those desperate to have their names attached to a fundraising event. Small wonder that the celebs thought, to hell with it, and have gone ahead with their charity concerts and balls anyway.

It was on 4 January that Médecins Sans Frontières issued its statement. At that point, the reaction of the British public to the tsunami disaster had been admirable. It had been rapid, generous and anonymous. Since then, however, tsunami mania has become a little nauseating. The disaster is no longer about Indonesians losing their families, their homes, their livelihoods; it is about minor celebs battling it out to see who cares most.

After 9/11 [the September 11, 2001, terrorist attacks on America] there was a fashion for cancelling parties, dinners and even football matches as 'a mark of respect'. For the tsunami, on the other hand, such puritanical gestures have been discarded; rather the deaths of some 225,000 people have sparked off a party season such as London has seldom seen in the middle of January. On Sunday 23 January, for example, for the price of £100 a couple, you could have waltzed on down to the 'Emergency Party' at the 20th-Century Theatre in Westbourne Grove, sponsored by Burberry and organised by something called the Bayswater Tsunami Appeal.

The Use of Charity for Self-Promotion
There is nothing on the invitation to say exactly how the money raised will be spent, though there is enough room to print the names of the extensive organising committee, including Rosie

Supporting a Cause Because of a Celebrity

Have you ever gotten more information or done anything to support a cause because of something you heard an actor, singer, or other celebrity say or do?

		Generation/Age			
	Total	**Echo Boomers (18–31)**	**Gen X (32–43)**	**Baby Boomers (44–62)**	**Matures (63+)**
		Percentage			
Yes	15	17	19	18	7
No	85	83	81	82	93

Taken from: The Harris Poll #43, Harris Interactive, April 17, 2008.
www.harrisinteractive.com/harris_poll/printerfriend/index.asp?PID=897.

Boycott, Geordie Greig and Gabriella Windsor. If you are a celeb and you didn't manage to get your name associated with that event, don't worry: there is always the Tsunami Appeal Celebrity Dinner on 31 January at the Intercontinental Hotel, featuring an auction of promises including a riding lesson from Richard Dunwoody, a DIY [do it yourself] makeover from Tommy Walsh and, top of the bill, dinner with Michael Portillo. Great though the suffering of the Indonesians is, it must be reassuring for them to know there will always be someone on Earth worse off than themselves.

Here's a test to see how strong a stomach you have: read this extract from NBC News on 12 January and see if you can keep your breakfast down: 'Tom Cruise, Jamie Foxx, Virginia Madsen, David Duchovny, Tim Robbins and all the other celebs who were part of the Critics' Choice Awards on Monday are donating their gift bags to raise money for tsunami relief. The bags are huge sports bags jammed with gift certificates for everything from clothes to relaxation, and tickets to the Indy 500. They are now up for auction on eBay along with photos of each celeb autographing or standing with his or her gift bags. . . .' Gee, how very generous: to give away the bag of freebies which has just been stuffed under your nose at some awards dinner.

It isn't just the big stars, however. Just about every wannabe in Britain has latched on to the promotional possibilities of raising cash for tsunami victims. Take this gem—one of literally hundreds to be found on the Internet advertising tsunami events at the nation's pubs and clubs—about a party at the Chapel Bar in Islington and listed on the website of Virtual Festivals, which promotes live music events: 'Sara Bowrey has decided to let us donate her birthday party to help raise funds the best way we know how: by putting on a full day of live bands and inviting you to join us in a celebration of great music. . . . All money raised will go to the Unicef tsunami children's fund—and we will have a BBC2 film crew with us all day to capture the fun.' For all I know, Ms Bowrey may have dug deep into her own pockets, but lots of other people have done so, many of them poor pensioners on a few pounds a week. It is just that none of the others thought about donating their birthday party as well. Just how does one 'donate' a birthday party? Ms Bowrey got her friends round for a dance, just as she would have done had there been no tsunami. But on top of it she got the chance to take the credit for other people's generosity—and get a plug on BBC2 to boot!

Celebrities have always attended charity events, but it wasn't until Bob Geldof's first Band Aid single in 1984 that it became an indispensable rite of celebritydom to get your face associated with fundraising. Geldof, though, did his research and used his celebrity to draw attention to a disaster which might otherwise have passed many people by. Not so the assorted luvvies and popsters who have jumped on the tsunami bandwagon. By the time the first celebs were showing the world just how much they cared, a well-funded rescue mission was already under way.

Tsunami Bandwagon Distracts from Other Worthy Causes

One imagines that the money raised by celebs over the past few weeks [in January 2005] will be put to some good use, even if it is in adorning Phuket's rebuilt hotels in gold leaf. But the problem with the tsunami bandwagon is that it distracts from equally worthy causes. Why can't just one of these celebrity events home in on the world's other horrors? The organisers wouldn't have to look far for ideas. The Médecins Sans Frontières website no longer has a box asking for donations for the tsunami appeal. Instead, it lists what it describes as the 'top ten under-reported humanitarian stories from 2004'. Among the victims who won't be supported at this month's gala dinners are the 1.6 million Ugandans displaced by the Lord's Resistance Army, the 150,000 rural peoples of the Congo displaced by civil war, the 300,000 Liberians who have yet to return to their homes after the civil war there, the Chechens who have been bombed out of their homes by Russian forces—an oppression which [British prime minister] Tony Blair regards as [Russian prime minister] Vladimir Putin's contribution to the war on terror.

In simpler ages, people at the heart of a natural or man-made humanitarian crisis might have looked to the gods, or to the British empire. Nowadays, it would be more profitable to look for a Hollywood agent—and just hope that your crisis is bigger, better and more deserving of Kate Winslet's ball-gown than the next country's crisis.

THIRTEEN

Pride Parades Are an Important Part of Gay Activism

Carlos Santoscoy

Carlos Santoscoy, managing editor and publisher of On Top magazine, originally intended the following selection to be the magazine's annual, dutiful piece on the importance of Gay Pride events. But his message became more pressing after a 2007 attack on gay activists in Moscow. The attacks were a reminder that achieving gay rights has been a hard-fought battle and that Gay Pride events are an important way to celebrate the movement's progress. On Top magazine is an online magazine that describes itself as a gay advocacy Web site.

It's Pride time and our opinion piece was going to be another attempt to convey the spirit of Pride and the reasons why it even matters in 2007. We were feeling this would be an uphill battle. You see Pride in America is now taken for granted. Another parade, another festival. Do we need to see Dykes on Bykes . . . again?

Then this happened: The AP [Associated Press] wire service on May 27th [2007] reported that Gay Pride supporters in Moscow were attacked, insulted, egg-tossed, and punched and kicked on their way to hand over a memorandum signed by more than 40 members of the European Parliament requesting permission to hold a gay pride march in central Moscow to mayor Yuri Luzhkov.

Carlos Santoscoy, "Why Gay Pride Matters," On Top magazine, May 28, 2007. Reproduced by permission.

Mr. Luzhkov already had banned any such demonstration and earlier had described Gay Pride marches as a "work of Satan." Both the attackers and demonstrators were arrested by police who intervened much later.

BBC News quoted gay rights activist Peter Tatchell as saying, "We were violently assaulted—I was battered in the face and the eye, and knocked to the ground, kicked and beaten. The Moscow police, astonishingly, arrested me and let my attackers walk free."

In Russia homosexuality is blamed for a raft of social ills. Russian president Vladamir Putin has blamed it for a declining birth rate. New legislation introduced last week [May 2007] seeks to pull back the curtain of progress to Stalin-era criminalization of homosexuality.

Remember Stonewall?

Yet, were we not in this position in 1969 when the Stonewall riots began? It is difficult to believe that in the mid 60's people were routinely arrested, their only crime being present in a gay bar during a police raid. During these raids police would often beat-up any resistors. Homosexuality was illegal in most states.

Then on June 28th 1969 the patrons of the Stonewall Inn in New York City fought back against the police. The Stonewall

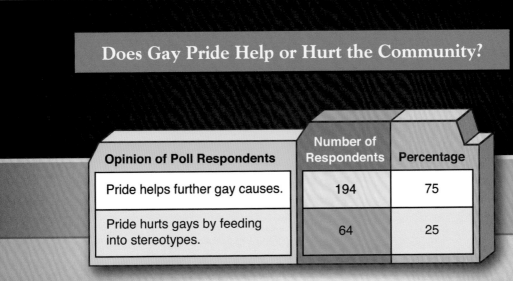

Does Gay Pride Help or Hurt the Community?

Opinion of Poll Respondents	Number of Respondents	Percentage
Pride helps further gay causes.	194	75
Pride hurts gays by feeding into stereotypes.	64	25

Taken from: "Gay Life," About.com, January 21, 2009.
http://gaylife.about.com/gi/pages/poll.htm?poll_id–6579420034&linkback–.

Inn had had a long history of being raided by the police, probably due to its mainly transgender and drag queen clientèle. Yet during this raid the drag queens resisted. The ensuing riot, which lasted several days and included as many as 2000 demonstrators at its height, has often been given credit as the flash point that sparked the modern Gay Liberation Movement.

It is ironic, even comical, to think that the farthest fringe element of gay society, often cited as the weakest link in our gay chain, the effeminate man who never denied his gay identity was the first to stand up and resist while the Rock Hudsons [a gay actor] of the world remained quiet and hidden.

For the gay community, Gay Pride parades, such as this one in New York City, are an important way of celebrating the progress of their movement.

Gay Pride Celebrates Our Progress

Gay Pride around the world celebrates the progress the movement has achieved since Stonewall, we have gained the right to free assembly, but full equality remains an elusive goal. Yet as we gained tangible rights, visibility, and even acceptance the Gay Pride event has come under attack as a distraction, an over commercialized event ripe with images that inevitably our foes use against us.

While today's [May 28, 2007,] event is more commercial than political, ask Moscow mayor Yuri Luzhkov if a commercial version of a Gay Pride parade would be more acceptable for his city? It would not be, you see what makes our enemies cringe is the fact that Gay Pride exists at all, the event *is* the political statement. The inescapable truth is that Gay Pride is more than a parade or festival but a spirit of resistance, and while its images of leather daddies, drag queens, and Dykes on Bykes may provide fodder for our foes, for the gay community it provides a healthy dose of . . . wait for it . . . pride!

FOURTEEN

Gay Pride Activists Should Focus on Civil Rights, Not Fringe Groups

Keith W. Swain

> Keith W. Swain argues in the following selection that gay pride needs a new direction. In his opinion, events like Gay Pride marches focus too much attention on fringe groups, like drag queens or fetish groups. He writes of the PrideFest parade in Denver: "In its attempt to meet the needs of such a diverse community, it tries to be everything to everyone. Sadly as a result, it has become nothing to anyone." Events like PrideFest, argues Swain, pull the attention away from the most important issue gay people face—gaining equality under the law. Swain is a psychotherapist and former director of the Gay and Lesbian Community Center of Colorado.

Denver's gay pride parade is heading from Cheesman Park down Colfax Avenue to the Civic Center today [June 21, 2007]. But, honestly, I think the whole event is heading in the wrong direction.

Don't get me wrong. I am, and have been all my life, a supporter of the gay rights movement. As a gay man, how could I not be? I fully support the movement's belief that we all have the right to live free from government interference and organized social oppression. But one of the greatest tools of the movement, pride marches (and maybe even the movement itself) have been hijacked by the "sex" in sexual orientation.

Originally, the intent of the gay civil rights movement was pretty simple: It was wrong to be treated any differently than the rest of the citizenry because one was different—be it skin color, religious choice, or sexual orientation.

But over the years, that simplicity has grown complex, through a loving yet misguided attempt at non-judgmental inclusion. As a result, the current "community" is now a growing cluster of people with virtually nothing in common other than being part of a sexual minority.

I can understand the movement's focus on sex issues in the early days, as the most pressing concern facing the community at the time were anti-sodomy laws. The lives of thousands of gay

American Attitudes on Gay Marriage

U.S. adults are now about evenly divided on whether they support allowing gay and lesbian couples to legally marry.

Favor
47 percent

Oppose
49 percent

Taken from: "Pulse of Equality Study," Harris Interactive, December 3, 2008. www.glaad.org/media/release_detail.php?id=4842.

men and women were destroyed by the abuse of these laws. But we are in a very different place today. According to FreedomToMarry .org, there are no states where gay sex is illegal, but 43 states where gay marriage is banned.

Nothing reflects this growing transformation of the gay rights movement into the sexual minority movement than the use of acronyms to describe this group. What once was known simply as the gay community became the lesbian and gay community, followed by the addition of the bisexual community and then the transsexual community. Obviously too long a term to say, it quickly became an acronym, the LGBT community. Yet, the trend of inclusion continues, as some call for adding those who are questioning and unsure or, as we would say, the LGBTQU [lesbian, gay, bisexual, transgender, questioning, and unsure] community. Is there no end?

The magazine *Anything That Moves* went so far as to call for the term FABGLITTER to stand for the Fetish, Allies, Bisexual, Gay, Lesbian, Intersexed, Transgender, Transsexual, Engendering Revolution.

At the risk of being considered politically incorrect: Enough, already.

Too Much Diversity Is Diluting the Gay Rights Movement

Reflecting the growing dilution of the gay rights movement in the name of diversity, Denver's PrideFest, of which the gay pride parade is a part, and the other pride marches across the country have followed the trend and have lost their ability to educate the public about the general gay community. PrideFest now is part protest, part parade, part political theater, part circuit party, and part street fair. In other words, in its attempt to meet the needs of such a diverse community, it tries to be everything to everyone. Sadly, as a result, it has become nothing to anyone, except the sexual fringe communities. The gay men and women I know stay away from PrideFest, not out of discomfort for being gay, but because current PrideFest participants are not reflective of them or their values.

Some people argue that Gay Pride parades have lost their ability to educate the public because they have come to resemble part political theater and part street fair for the sexual fringe groups of the movement.

There have been attempts to change the path of gay pride. In 1984, I was director of the Gay and Lesbian Community Center of Colorado. My staff and I asked the question "What is our intended message?" It was a time when the gay community was being decimated by the growing number of AIDS deaths. We suggested a mourners march, complete with black clothes, a single drummer, a bagpiper, something to show the city we were hurting, grieving, dying daily. Community organizers and businesspeople rejected the idea. "What fun would that be? Besides, what would the drag queens wear?"

So today, we have a sexy party instead of a political statement. Yet, the sexual concerns of the early gay movement have been met. What is lost in all the glitter, feathers and leather harnesses of PrideFest is the power to move the public to better understand gay men and women. The sexual revolution is over, yet PrideFest lingers in that adolescent sexual environment of the '70s and '80s. Frankly, those sexual displays at PrideFest tend to do more damage than good.

Gay women and men in Colorado face discrimination every day, in employment, in housing, in public accommodation, and in legal recognition of our relationships. So why all the focus on sexual inclusion?

The gay community must put away the whips and gowns and get serious about the powerful impact PrideFest can have on our futures. It's time to disengage from the fringe sexual communities and instead focus on the real needs of gay men and women in Colorado. It's time to discourage the overt sexual displays of the poly-amorous, the drag queens, and the fetish communities. If and when it becomes illegal to be bisexual or to dress as a woman, I'll join that protest parade. But for now, it is essential that our PrideFest message be strong, simple, and about one community with one issue: the equality of gay men and women.

FIFTEEN

Nonviolent Activism Is Key to a Stable Future

Rolf Carriere and Michael Nagler

> The following is an argument in favor of nonviolent activism. Written by two longtime peace activists, Rolf Carriere and Michael Nagler, the piece points to the ways in which nonviolence is used as a safe and successful form of activism. Unarmed peacekeepers throughout the world have rescued child soldiers, protected villages, and monitored elections, they write, citing Mohandas Gandhi's words that nonviolence is "the greatest force mankind has been endowed with." The authors are senior advisers to Nonviolent Peaceforce. Carriere is a former UNICEF [United Nations Children's Fund] liaison to the World Bank. Nagler is professor emeritus of Peace and Conflict Studies at the University of California–Berkeley.

Legends relate that Buddha stopped a war between two kings who were quarreling over rights to a river by asking them, "Which is more precious, blood or water?"

Could ordinary people use the same kind of wisdom—and courage—to check the impulse to fight wars today—over oil, water, or identity? Mahatma Gandhi thought so. He created teams of civilians called the Shanti Sena or "Army of Peace" and deployed them in various communities around India where they could avert communal riots and provide other peacekeeping services.

Rolf Carriere and Michael Nagler, "Fight Violence with Nonviolence," *Christian Science Monitor*, March 27, 2008. Reproduced by permission of the authors.

Mohandas Gandhi is considered the father of nonviolent civil disobedience, and his teachings influenced Martin Luther King, Jr. to adopt nonviolent tactics in the civil rights movement.

Over the past 25 years nonviolent peacekeepers have been going into zones of sometimes intense conflict with the aim of bringing a measure of peace, protection, and sanity to life there. Rather than use threat or force, unarmed peacekeepers deploy strategies of protective accompaniment, moral and/or witnessing "presence," monitoring election campaigns, creating neutral safe spaces, and in extreme cases putting themselves physically between hostile parties, as Buddha did with the angry kings in ancient India.

Civilian unarmed peacekeeping has had dramatic, small-scale, quiet, and unglamorous successes: rescuing child soldiers, protecting the lives of key human rights workers and of whole villages, averting potentially explosive violence, and generally raising the level of security felt by citizens in many a tense community.

A Nonviolence Success Story

Recently a village on the island of Mindanao in the Philippines was under threat by two armed groups who had come within 200 meters of each other. The village elders called for help from the Nonviolent Peaceforce stationed there, who intervened and by communicating with all sides persuaded the armed group to back away. Thanks to mediation, no violence erupted, no lives were lost.

Why haven't you heard about this exciting work? Because it is terribly underfunded, for one thing. There is also a prevailing prejudice that only governments or armed forces—including those of the United Nations [UN]—have the responsibility or means to contain conflict. While the UN Security Council has often authorized "all necessary means" to maintain peace and prevent violent conflict, in fact, the UN has not systematically considered large-scale civilian unarmed peacekeeping.

But the biggest obstacle by far is the widespread—and rarely examined—belief that political power grows out of the barrel of a gun. It is the belief that there is only one kind of power; threat power, which in the end can be relied upon to get others to change their minds or, failing that, at least their actions.

That may change. The failures of war-fighting for peace, most notably now in Iraq, are getting ever more costly—of life, material, and our civil liberties.

Nonviolent Peacekeeping Is the Future

The new global norm of "Responsibility to Protect" (R2P) should inspire the use of civil society and nonviolent means. While it includes military interventions, R2P is based on emerging international human security and human rights doctrine that aims to avert further failure by the international community to prevent and stop genocide, war crimes, ethnic cleansing, and crimes against humanity.

It may yet dawn on the world that these courageous nonviolent peacekeepers are not "unarmed;" they are armed with what Gandhi made bold to call "the greatest force mankind has been endowed with"—nonviolence.

Nonviolent Peaceforce is working to bring this kind of peacekeeping to greater prominence, with the goal of increasing its current 70 field team members to a cadre of 2,000 by 2012. For a

Potential International Benefits of the Proposed U.S. Department of Peace

The Department of Peace will:

- Advise the president, the secretaries of defense and state, and others on root causes of violence, plus practical ways to dismantle violence while still in a formative phase

- Support the military by:

  - Providing cultural, ethnic, and psychologically insightful information, education, and technology

  - Offering practical skills (such as conflict resolution techniques) for the amelioration of violence among adversarial factions

  - Administering the training and support of civilian peacekeepers for participation in multinational, nonviolent peace forces

recent deployment, Nonviolent Peaceforce had applicants hailing from 55 countries for every position available.

Well-trained unarmed civilians are saving lives and protecting communities under threat in some of the world's most violent places. They are growing. Recently the Geneva-based Centre for Humanitarian Dialogue issued a study documenting how and why this type of "proactive presence" works.

People are ready for peaceful change and they're willing to dedicate their lives to create it. Civilian unarmed peacekeeping could be *the* way to recognize and help develop the vital protection role global civil society may credibly, effectively, and legitimately play in human security. For the benefit of children and women in armed conflict, for refugees, journalists, human rights defenders, peacefully protesting monks, aid workers, or election campaigners—for all of us. Because ultimately, none of us is secure until all of us are.

SIXTEEN

Nonviolence Does Not Work

Daniel Greenfield

In the following selection Daniel Greenfield argues that nonviolence is useless as a political tool. Not only is nonviolence ineffective, he writes, but it is part of a harmful "pacifist strain" that runs through Western civilization. "It is a particularly futile and dangerous strain that values internal nobility over the lives and welfare of others," he writes. Furthermore, he argues, nonviolence is useless against truly tyrannical opponents because they cannot be shamed into choosing a less violent path. Greenfield is a political writer and commentator who focuses on the war on terror.

[Mohandas] Gandhi's tactic of non-violence is often foolishly credited with the peaceful liberation of India. This claim would be more impressive if the British Empire hadn't expired but was still around with a large retinue of colonies, instead of having disposed of its colonies, many around the same time as India. And considering the bloodshed of Partition [the dividing of India into sovereign states in 1947], despite Gandhi's best attempts at appeasing Muslims it was hardly peaceful. Yet despite the hypocrisies that have dotted Gandhi's life, his ideas continue to have a powerful hold on the Western imagination.

Daniel Greenfield, "Why Gandhi Was Wrong—Non-Violence Doesn't Work," *Canada Free Press*, August 2008.

Few would seriously argue that had Gandhi been facing Imperial Japan (whose brutal conquest of Asia he briefly supported) or Nazi Germany or even the British Empire of the 19th century, that non-violence would have been nothing more than an invitation to a bullet. Yet that is exactly what first world nations are expected to do when confronted with terrorism. Not long after 9/11 [September 11, 2001, terrorist attacks on America] slogans were already appearing on posters challenging, "What would Gandhi do?"

We can hazard a guess at what the man who urged Britain to surrender to [Adolf] Hitler and told the Jews to walk into the gas chambers, would do. We can do better than guess at the outcome. The same outcome that surrenders to tyranny always brings, whether in the name of non-violence, cowardice or political appeasement, a great heap of skulls shining in the sun.

Gandhi's non-violence or [author Leo] Tolstoy's more honestly named Non-Resistance to Evil through Violence, [which] heavily influenced Gandhi, or Tolstoy's own influence through the writings of [philosopher Jean-Jacques] Rousseau represent a pacifist strain that runs through Western civilization. It is a particularly futile and dangerous strain that values internal nobility over the lives and welfare of others.

Non-violence Is Redundant

Non-violence is either redundant or dangerously misguided. When confronting an opponent, that opponent's goals are either violent or peaceful. If his goals are peaceful then non-violence is redundant. If his goals are violent, then non-violence achieves nothing. The political victories of non-violence have come mainly from a nation that wanted a peaceful outcome seeing violent suppression of protesters through violent law enforcement tactics. While this produced political victories, it also demonstrated the inherent pointless[ness] of it, as it only worked with a nation that was already prepared to reach a peaceful agreement.

Had Martin Luther King tried his tactics in the early 19th century South, he would have gotten nowhere. Had Gandhi pitted himself against Imperial Japan, he would have been beheaded. Clearly non-violence is a tactic that can only work against essentially peaceful opponents who are easily embarrassed by a few jailed protesters. It fails utterly against opponents who genuinely want to conquer or kill you and are willing to do whatever it takes to see that it happens.

Had the application of non-violence been limited to a form of civil protest in democracies, there would be no objection. It is when Gandhi is cited as a model for confronting dictatorships and tyrannies that we reach the fundamental gap between reality and the ideology of non-violence.

Can non-violence stop an enemy bent on your destruction? The answer is no. Non-violence can only enable such an enemy. But the nasty trap in the philosophy of non-violence is that it presumes that a source of the violence is in the victims themselves.

This is why when Gandhi advised the Jews to go willingly into the gas chambers, he described any protest by the Jews to the West as itself violent. Only by being willing, unprotesting sacrifices could the Jews fit Gandhi's model of non-violence. This is shocking only to those who fail to realize that "Blame the Victim" is inherent in the philosophy of non-violence. Unsurprising from a man who degraded and abused his wife and drove his sons away, and yet continues to be regarded as a sort of saint.

Non-violence Is Self-Destructive

The self-destructive nature of non-violence is that it only works when the source of the violence really is within the individual practicing it. Non-violence only works therefore when non-violently confronting those whose goals are ultimately non-violent. It is self-destructively useless when confronting those whose goals are violent. But because it teaches that we are the source of the violence, it repeatedly blames the target of the violence for doing anything whatsoever to resist the violence.

Advocates of nonviolent protest, such as Gandhi, Tolstoy, and Martin Luther King, Jr., were influenced by the writings of French philosopher Jean-Jacques Rousseau (1712–1788), pictured.

In Gandhi's non-violence, a rape victim who screamed for help would be guilty of practicing violence rather than non-violence. In Tolstoy's rendering of non-violence, there is no difference in moral culpability between attacked and attacker. This simplistic picture leaves no room for self-defense and no place for a society that seeks to protect its own people. When viewed this way it exposes the ideology of non-violence for what it really is, a self-indulgent selfish form of martyrdom that emphasizes inner nobility over social utility.

At the heart of non-violence is hypocrisy. Quaker non-violence prevented them from funding a militia to protect colonial settlers against attacks. It prevented them from serving on either side in WW2 [World War II]. It did not however prevent them from composing lists of victims for the Nazis. It has not prevented them from agitating on behalf of terrorists today.

Tolstoy's non-violence did not prevent him from distributing and promoting the writings of violent anarchists; it did however prevent him from condemning the Pogroms [persecutions of Jews]. Gandhi's non-violence did not prevent him from self-interestedly welcoming a Japanese occupation of Asia or urging a British surrender to Hitler.

The common denominator of non-violence is a contempt for the victim of violence and a slavish need to appease or appeal to the violent. Given a choice non-violence will elevate the perpetrator of naked violence, over the peace-loving people and

The hot new video game where you're a peacemaker who disarms everyone in sight and sells them on the virtues of nonviolent communication.

Cartoon by Jason Love, www.CartoonStock.com.

nations doing their best to stop him. The former has the glory of an unambiguous sinner ripe for conversion, while the latter appears to the philosopher of non-violence as an obscene heresy that uses violence to achieve peaceful ends.

For the democracy confronting a destructive ideology, non-violence is nothing more than a suicide pact. The refusal to resist evil grants hegemony to evil. But the refusal of the philosophers of non-violence to admit the necessity of violence instead drives them to demonize those who would resist evil with violence, as the source of the violence.

What You Should Know About Activism

Facts About Activism

- Activism is taking some sort of intentional action to support a particular social or political cause. Activist acts encompass anything from buying greener products, to writing a letter to the editor of a newspaper, to staging a major political rally.

- The most important issues to students, according to the annual *Mother Jones* Student Activism survey, are human rights (40 percent), the environment and global warming (29 percent), and ending poverty (12 percent).

- A 2006 study from the Corporation for National and Community Service (CNCS), a federal agency that oversees service programs, found that 15.5 million teens aged twelve to eighteen volunteered with an organization, giving more than 1.3 billion hours of service in 2004.

- Volunteering by sixteen- to nineteen-year-olds more than doubled from 1989 to 2005, according to the CNCS study.

- The largest service event in the world is Global Youth Service (GYS) Day, an event held each April to educate the public on the contributions of youth volunteers and to celebrate and mobilize youth volunteers. Participants celebrate by doing a service project geared to their community's specific needs. According to Youth Service America, GYS Day has brought together over 73 million people in thousands of communities worldwide. Service projects have included 4-H volunteers in Kansas doing chores for senior citizens, teens in Thailand hosting a weeklong camp for children orphaned by AIDS, and youth in Bolivia teaching people how to disinfect their drinking water.

- *WireTap* magazine's Top Activism Victory of 2008 was the youth voter turnout in the presidential election. "23 million young people came out to vote on November 4th—the largest number since 1972 and 3.4 million more than in 2004," reported the magazine.

Youth Activism and History

- Early in American history, youth activism was fairly rare, although it did occur, according to historian Steven Novak. During Revolutionary times, students at Princeton hanged in effigy politicians sympathetic to England.
- Mary Harris "Mother" Jones, a staunch advocate of child labor laws, led an early U.S. youth activist movement. In 1903 she marched one hundred thousand child coal miners and mill workers to Washington, D.C., carrying signs that read, "We want to go to school and not the mines."
- The earliest large youth organization in America, according to YouthRights.net, was the American Youth Congress (AYC). The AYC was formed in 1934 to address problems facing young people and was supported by First Lady Eleanor Roosevelt. In 1936 the group issued the Declaration of Rights of American Youth, which asked for "full educational opportunities, steady employment at adequate wages, security in time of need, civil rights, religious freedom, and peace."
- The Students for a Democratic Society (SDS) was a milestone in 1960s youth activism. The group, which held its first meeting in Ann Arbor, Michigan, in 1960, issued the Port Huron Statement, a paper that listed the organization's priorities, including workers' rights and ending racial discrimination and nuclear proliferation. On April 26, 1968, as part of a "Ten Days of Resistance" campaign, over a million students skipped school for one day, the then-largest student strike in U.S. history.

School and Community Activism

- Students who participate in service learning, an educational method that connects community service to classroom learning, were less likely to get in trouble, had better school attendance, felt more connected to their community, and even had higher test scores, according to the Corporation for National and Community Service.

- According to the Higher Education Research Institute at UCLA, growing numbers of high school seniors (83.3 percent) volunteer for various causes, up from 66 percent in 1989. And, although many high schools now require students to do community service, 70 percent of the high school volunteers were not required to do so.

- Since 1993 over half a million people have served in Americorps, a national service organization. Americorps places volunteers aged seventeen and older with groups such as Habitat for Humanity, the Red Cross, and Boys and Girls Clubs of America. Members who complete their ten- to-twelve-month service period receive $4,725 to use for college.

- Pay It Forward, a group that facilitates students spending their spring breaks doing community service projects, has grown from forty-three participants in 2004 to about eight hundred in 2008, according to *USA Today*.

- The National Honor Society, the organization that recognizes outstanding high school and middle school students, requires its members to work on a service project selected by their local chapter. Other chapters may also require that members perform a certain number of hours on individual service projects. Each year the Top Ten National Student Volunteers, ranging from age twelve to eighteen, are given five-thousand-dollar personal awards and five thousand dollars to donate to the charity of their choice.

Activism and the Internet

- Activist social networks are gaining in popularity but are still relatively small scale. Idealist, a service-oriented site, has 178,000 active members, and the environmental site WiserEarth has 21,000. Facebook, by contrast, has 150 million active users.

- DoSomething.org is the largest online teen service organization. Each month the site gets over six hundred thousand hits, according to DoSomething.
- In the Mother Jones survey, 49 percent of students and 46 percent of nonstudents considered Facebook to be the future of activism.
- MySpace has over twenty-eight thousand nonprofit and philanthropic groups listed.
- Facebook has 445 results using the search terms "activist groups." Of these, many include groups with titles like "Joining Facebook groups does not make you a political activist."
- The top 5 Facebook advocacy groups are Reduce the Drinking Age to 18!, Legalize Same-Sex Marriage, Americans for Alternative Energy, Support a Woman's Right to Choose, and Support Stem Cell Research.

What You Should Do About Activism

Activism. The word means different things to different people. When you hear it, maybe you picture a protest rally or someone handing out leaflets. Some may have positive associations and imagine someone admirable working hard on an honorable cause. Others may recoil, picturing an overly zealous volunteer trying to usurp the status quo.

Whether or not we realize it, we are all activists. Whenever we speak our mind on an issue, support a cause, or donate our time, we are performing activist acts. Even buying a product can be an activist act. Choosing organic, grass-fed beef from a local butcher, buying a veggie burger, or picking up cheap burgers at a fast food chain each plays different parts in determining what kind of a world we live in. In a sense, even doing nothing is an activist act. Doing nothing can be construed as an approval of the way things already are.

Activism Works

Some may wonder whether activism is worth it. Is having a demonstration an effective technique? Can handing out leaflets really help anything? Yes, activism does work. A University of Washington study analyzed environmental protests and changes in environmental law since 1960 to measure whether activism correlated with changes in the law. The researchers found that each protest increased the chances of pro-environmental legislation being passed by 1.2 percent. Moderate protest increased the annual rate of adoption by 9.5 percent. Surprisingly, protest was much more effective in shaping environmental policy than expensive lobbying from large environmental organizations.

Activists started the United States, and activists have been helping shape the country ever since. "If we make a list of the major advances in democratic society from the right to vote, for example, all the way to the fruits of a democratic society, we will see that the initiative started almost always by one or a handful of citizens who decided to stand tall," wrote consumer activist Ralph Nader in his essay "Developing a Civic Culture." Activists have been crucial in practically everything that shapes our lives, from food safety rules, to ending child labor in the United States to getting seat belts in cars. Activism shapes the big things in our lives and the small things. The TV show *Family Guy* returned, not once, but twice, after being canceled because disappointed fans became activists and demanded that Fox bring the show back. (Meanwhile activists on the other side of the debate have brought out a petition seeking to cancel the show, charging it with being an unoriginal *Simpsons* rip-off).

Finding a Way into Activism

"We are the ones we've been waiting for. We are the change that we seek," said then senator Barack Obama in a speech on the 2008 presidential campaign trail, urging his supporters to action. People, regular people, are integral in creating what the future will be like. No matter what, change is going to happen. And the only way to affect the results is to play a part in making the changes.

How do people become activists? For some, circumstances in their lives spur them into action. Someone whose relative is stricken by a disease may decide that they will work to fight that disease. Others just decide they want to give something back to the world. Still others find a situation so unjust or so unacceptable that they are forced to do something about it.

Everyone will find that certain issues are closer to their heart than others. Your job is to find the things that you are most passionate about. These may or may not be the same things that your family or friends care about the most. No matter what other people think, you should choose issues that are important to you. Your activism will be much more rewarding if you pick a cause that you feel passionate about (and you will probably be a better worker for the cause, too).

In your own life as an activist, you can do as little or as much as you want. For some, buying green products may be a small, initial step. Or simply joining a Facebook cause may be the way you start. Others will be so dedicated to changing the world that they will become lifelong activists, either as volunteers or as an employee of an organization.

A good way to discover the kind of cause you might like to work on is to take a look around you. What are the problems you see in your school or community? Are there local organizations that you really believe in? Are you interested in championing the rights of elderly people, the environment, pets, kids, poor people, or something else? If you see a problem and there is not a group working on it, consider starting your own group. Teens are especially good activists because they have good ideas and lots of energy. Plus, newspapers and other media outlets love stories of enterprising teens making a difference.

The Internet is another excellent route to finding avenues for activism. Web sites like Youth Noise (www.youthnoise.org) and Do Something (http://dosomething.org) explain different causes and offer networking, training, and ways to get involved.

A Little Effort Makes a Huge Difference

Small actions can make a huge difference. Something as simple as writing a letter to the editor of a newspaper, for example, can easily get your viewpoint out to thousands of people—and perhaps change some minds. Also effective is writing a letter to your state, local, or national legislator. According to former congressperson Billy Evan (D-GA), "Legislators estimate that 10 letters from constituents represent the concerns of 10,000 citizens. Anybody who will take the time to write is voicing the fears and desires of thousands more." (Because of the volume of letters national leaders receive, your letter-writing talents might be best used on letters to local officials, who get less feedback from constituents.)

The good thing about activism is that it can be tailored to each person's life and interests. Writers can be activists through their work, as can artists, dancers, and musicians. Teachers, city officials, and Parent-Teacher Association, or PTA, members are activists. Activism can make the best use of what talents you have. Sports fans could host an all-star game to raise funds for a charity, social types could throw a party to raise awareness for a cause, and class clowns might consider creating clever stunts to highlight a particular issue. There is no limit to what kinds of ideas you can dream up—and no limit to the changes you can make.

The editors have compiled the following list of organizations concerned with the issues debated in this book. The descriptions are derived from materials provided by the organizations. All have publications or information available for interested readers. The list was compiled on the date of publication of the present volume; the information provided here may change. Be aware that many organizations take several weeks or longer to respond to inquiries, so allow as much time as possible.

Do Something
24–32 Union Square East, 4th Fl., New York, NY 10003
(212) 254-2390
e-mail: mstevenson@dosomething.org
Web site: http://dosomething.org

Do Something is a teen-focused organization that provides social action training, clubs, and social action boot camp. The Web site features tools and information for teens to decide which causes to support and easy ways to get involved in social action projects.

The Freechild Project
PO Box 6185, Olympia, WA 98507-6185
(360) 753-2686
e-mail: info@freechild.org
Web site: www.freechild.org

The Freechild Project's mission is to advocate, inform, and celebrate social change led by and with young people around the world, particularly those who have been historically denied the right to participate. The group's Web site offers information on social issues and how youth can and have become involved. The Freechild Project publishes *The Freechild Project* newsletter.

Global Action Youth Network (GYAN)
33 Flatbush Ave., 5th Fl., Brooklyn, NY 11217
(212) 661-611
e-mail: gyan@youthlink.org
Web site: www.youthink.org

GYAN is a youth-led organization that facilitates the efforts of young people working to improve the world and connects youth organizations worldwide. The organization's resources include Taking It Global (TIG), the largest worldwide social network for youth interested in social change. TIG offers an online community for activists, research, information on how to get involved with issues, and resources for teachers. GYAN publishes the *YouthLink Express* newsletter and *TIG* magazine.

Humane Teen
67 Norwich Essex Turnpike, East Haddam, CT 06423-1736
(860) 434-8666
e-mail: teens@humanesociety.org
Web site: www.humaneteen.org

Humane Teen, the youth branch of the Humane Society of the United States, seeks to educate young people about the importance of kindness to animals. The group's Web site offers animal rights news, profiles of teen activists, message boards, educational videos, and ways to get involved. It publishes the e-newsletter *Updates.*

Idealist
302 Fifth Ave., 11th Fl., New York, NY 10001
(212) 843-3973 • fax: (212) 695-7243
Web site: www.idealist.org/if/h

Idealist is a Web site project of the nonprofit group Action Without Borders. The Web Site offers volunteer opportunities, forums for debate, and tools for people interested in starting community actions.

International Lesbian, Gay, Bisexual, Transgender,
Queer Youth and Student Organisation (IGLYO)
Rue de la Charité 17, B-1012 Brussels, Belgium
e-mail: info@iglyo.com
Web site: www.iglyo.com

IGLYO is an umbrella organization for gay youth organizations
worldwide. IGLYO hosts conferences, offers anti-hate training,
and provides news and networking opportunities via its Web site.
IGLYO publishes the quarterly magazine *IGLYO on* . . . .

The National Youth Rights Association (NYRA)
1133 Nineteenth St. NW, 9th Fl., Washington, DC 20036
(202) 833-1200 x5714
e-mail: nyra@youthrights.org
Web site: www.youthrights.org

The NYRA defends the civil and human rights of young people in
the United States by educating people about youth rights, working with public officials, and empowering young people to work
on their own behalf. On its Web site NYRA highlights issues,
offers information, and mobilizes action campaigns. The group
publishes the monthly newsletter *NYRA Freedom*.

People for the Ethical Treatment of Animals (PETA)
501 Front St., Norfolk, VA 23510
(757) 622-7382 • fax: (757) 622-0457
e-mail: info@peta.org
Web site: www.peta.org

PETA is the largest animal rights organization in the world. It
works through public education, cruelty investigations, research,
animal rescue, legislation, special events, celebrity involvement,
and protest campaigns. It publishes the magazine *Animal Times*.

Underground Action Alliance (UAA)
PO Box 7591, Pittsburgh, PA 15213-9998
e-mail: info@undergroundactionalliance.org
Web site: http://undergroundactionalliance.org

The UAA encourages members of the punk rock community to become citizen-activists. The UAA Web site offers world news, ways to get involved, and resources for activists, including the Students' Rights Resource, which educates students about their constitutional rights and how to exercise and protect them in public schools. The UAA publishes the UAA Web-Zine.

Voices of Youth
125 Maiden Ln., 11th Fl., New York, NY 10038
(212) 686-5522 • fax: (212) 779-1679
e-mail: information@unicefusa.org
Web site: www.unicef.org/voy

The mission of Voices of Youth, which is part of the human rights organization UNICEF (United Nations Children's Fund) and specifically geared to young people, is to offer teens a safe place to explore, discuss, and partner on issues related to human rights and social change. The Voices of Youth Web site features information about causes, polls, videos, quizzes, and a place to chat with other teens around the world.

Youth Action International (YAI)
125 Park St., Ste. 450, Traverse City, MI 49684
(646) 274-1366 • fax (646) 514-1242
e-mail: info@peaceforkids.org
Web site: www.youthactioninternational.org/yai

YAI is a network of young people working to help other youth in Africa who are affected by war or other difficult circumstances. The group offers micro-loans, health care, and vocational training. YAI provides speakers and publishes an e-newsletter.

Youth Activism Project
PO Box E, Kensington, MD 20895
(301) 929-8808 • toll-free: (800) 543-7693
e-mail: info@youthactivismproject.org
Web site: http://youthactivism.com

The Youth Activism Project is a nonpartisan organization dedicated to getting young people involved with issues. The group gives youth activists free advice via a hotline (800-543-7693), trains adults in collaborating with young people, and provides a networking forum. The Youth Activism Project publishes books, including *No Kidding Around!*; an oral history of youth activists; and an e-newsletter, Youth Activism E-news.

Youth Noise
1255 Post St., Ste. 1120, San Francisco, CA 94109
(415) 346-4433
e-mail: support@youthnoise.org
Web site: www.youthnoise.com

Youth Noise is an activist organization that offers a social networking site for people under the age of twenty-seven who want to become involved in a cause. Its Web site offers space for blogging, places to click to help various causes, and areas for users to debate on controversial topics. The site has information about causes from tolerance to the environment and ways to get involved.

BIBLIOGRAPHY

Books

Jennifer Baumgardner, Amy Richards, and Winona LaDuke, *Grassroots: A Field Guide for Feminist Activism.* New York: Farrar, Straus & Giroux, 2005.

Diane L. Beers, *For the Prevention of Cruelty: The History and Legacy of Animal Rights Activism in the United States.* Athens, OH: Swallow, 2006.

Bill Clinton, *Giving: How Each of Us Can Change the World.* New York: Knopf, 2007.

Mikki Halpin, *It's Your World—If You Don't Like It, Change It: Activism for Teenagers.* New York: Simon Pulse, 2004.

Christopher Kush, *The One-Hour Activist: The 15 Most Powerful Actions You Can Take to Fight for the Issues and Candidates You Care About.* Hoboken, NJ: Jossey-Bass, 2004.

Barbara A. Lewis, *The Teen Guide to Global Actions: How to Connect with Others (Near & Far) to Create Social Change.* Minneapolis: Free Spirit, 2007.

Joan Minieri and Paul Getsos, *Tools for Radical Democracy: How to Organize for Power in Your Community.* Hoboken, NJ: Jossey-Bass, 2007.

MySpace Community and Jeca Taudte, *MySpace/OurPlanet: Change Is Possible.* New York: HarperTeen, 2008.

Michael Prokosch, Laura Raymond, and Naomi Klein, *The Global Activist's Manual: Local Ways to Change the World.* New York: Nation, 2002.

Rik Scarce, *Eco-Warriors: Understanding the Radical Environmental Movement.* Walnut Creek, CA: Left Coast, 2005.

Randy Shaw, *The Activist's Handbook: A Primer.* Berkeley and Los Angeles: University of California Press, 2001.

Linda and Tosh Sivertsen, *Generation Green: The Ultimate Teen Guide to Living an Eco-Friendly Life*. New York: Simon Pulse, 2008.

Jackie Waldman, *Teens with the Courage to Give: Young People Who Triumphed over Tragedy and Volunteered to Make a Difference*. San Francisco: Conari, 2000.

Periodicals

Q. Allan Broka, "Gay Shame Is a Drag," *Advocate*, June 20, 2006.

Custodeus, "Property Destruction Turns Up the Heat," *Earth First!* Mabon 2008.

Editorial Board, "PETA's Undercover Agents Deserve a Pat on the Back," *Austin (TX) Post-Bulletin*, October 25, 2008.

John Hagel and John Seely Brown, "Student Activism Can Change the World," *Business Week*, May 30, 2008.

Danna Harman, "Can Celebrities Really Get Results?" *Christian Science Monitor*, August 23, 2007.

John Hepburn, "30 Years of Peaceful Direct Action," *Nova*, October 2007.

Elizabeth Lanier, "Celebrities and Politics Don't Mix," *Norfolk (VA) Virginian-Pilot*, October 24, 2008.

Brendan O'Neill, "Greens Are the Enemies of Liberty," *Guardian* (Manchester, UK), July 15, 2008.

Will Potter, "The Chilling Effect," *Satya*, December 2006/January 2007.

Peter Schworm, "Students Switching Activism to Boardroom," *Boston Globe*, August 13, 2007.

Internet Sources

Earth First! "Direct Action Gets the Goods." www.earthfirstjournal.org/subsection.php?id=1.

Kate Jerman and Lluvia Mulvaney-Stanak, "Still Proud," Out in the Mountains, July 7, 2005. www.mountainpridemedia.org/oitm/issues/2005/07jul2005/editorial.htm.

Martin Kearns and Jonathan Schwarz, "Armchair Activism That Works," TomPaine.com, February 2, 2007. www.tompaine.com/articles/2007/02/02armchair_activism_that_works.php.

Elizabeth May, "How to Be an Activist," Sierra Club of Canada. www.sierraclub.ca/national/activist.html.

Chuck Norris, "If Democracy Doesn't Work, Try Anarchy," WorldNetDaily, November 17, 2008. www.wnd.com/index.php?fa=PAGE.view&pageid=81195.

Radical Def, "Pragmatic Gay Activists Tone Down Rhetoric," Daily Kos, November 22, 2008. www.dailykos.com/story/2008/11/22/11500/164/1015/665122.

Hugo Rifkind, "Student Activism Is Back," *Times* (London), February 16, 2009. http://women.timesonline.co.uk/tol/life_and_style/women/the_way_we_live/article5739655.ece.

Anna Robinson-Sweet, "Why Aren't Teens Politically Active?" NewsHour, August 10, 2005. www.pbs.org/newshour/extra/speakout/mystory/activist_8-11.html.

Bob Sorokanich, "Complexity of Issues Limits Student Activism," *Daily Orange*, February 19, 2007. http://media.www.dailyorange.com/media/storage/paper522/news/2007/02/19/Opinion/Complexity.Of.Issues.Limits.Student. Activism-2727613.shtml.

Stop Cal Vivisection, 36
Student Labor Action
  Movement (SLAM), 30–33
Surveys
  on amount of power/
    influence held by groups, *18*
  on animal rights, *27*
  on community service, *48*
  on future of activism, *34*
  on gay marriage, *83*
  on gay pride, *79*
  on most important issues to
    students, *10*
  on power of corporations, *17*
  on support for national
    service proposals, *56*
Swain, Keith W., 82

T
Tatchell, Peter, 79
Teachers

have right to express political
  beliefs in schools, 47, 58–63
should not express political
  beliefs in schools, 64–67
Theunissen, Frederic, 37–38
Tolstoy, Leo, 93, 95

U
UNICEF (United Nations
  International Children's
  Emergency Fund), 70, 72
University of California,
  Berkeley (UC Berkeley), 36
  campaign to stop vivisection
    at, 38–40

W
Weingarten, Randi, *62, 63*

Z
Zanca, Maria, 70, 72